'It just went like tinder' : *The mass movement & New Unionism in Britain 1889*

The Mass Movement and New Unionism in Britain 1889

'It just went like tinder'

a socialist history

John Charlton

'It just went like tinder': *The Mass Movement & New Unionism in Britain 1889*
John Charlton

First published September 1999

Redwords
1 Bloomsbury Street, London WC1B 3QE
www.fonseca.demon.co.uk

ISBN: 1 872208 11 8

Design and production: Roger Huddle and Rob Hoveman
Set in 12/15 Adobe Garamond
Printed by Larkham Printing and Publishing, London E3

Contents

REDWORDS operates as a publishing co-operative producing books, mainly cultural and historical, from a socialist perspective. We are linked to Bookmarks.

Redwords would like to thank
Chris Bambery
Hilary Chuter
Mac McKenna
Mary Phillips
Phil Whaite
for helping to publish this book

For Duncan Hallas

Acknowledgements

Special thanks are due to Chris Lloyd and Malcolm Barhamilton at Tower Hamlets Library, Ray Walker and Alain Kahan at the Working Class Movement Library in Salford who all searched enthusiastically for material, and the librarians at the TUC Library, University of North London, Hackney Archive (which houses the comprehensive Bryant & May papers) and the Fawcett Library who all gave meticulous personal assistance. The phrase 'Match Girls' can still open doors in archives and memory!

Comrades have also been exceptionally helpful, especially Rachel Aldred, Ian Birchall, Chris Bambery, Colin Barker, Ray Challinor and his excellent notes on the 1880s, Sybil Cock, Keith Flett, Donny Gluckstein, Duncan Hallas, Mike Haynes, Nick Howard, Sally Mitchison, Mary Perry, John Rees, Dave Tate, Duncan West and the London Socialist Historians 1998 Conference.

John Charlton, *July 1999*

Bibliography

All sources are listed in the endnotes. For anyone who wants to pursue the many stories involved the following books are a good start. Ken Coates and Tony Topham, *The Making of the Labour Movement,* London 1991, Anna Davin, *Growing Up Poor,* Cambridge 1997, Gareth Stedman Jones, *Outcast London,* London 1976, William J Fishman, *East End: 1888,* London 1988, and the same author's *East End Jewish Radicals: 1875-1914,* London 1975, Lynn Hollin Lees, *Exiles of Erin: Irish Migrants in Victorian London,* Lynn, Massachusetts 1979, and Joe White, *Tom Mann,* Manchester 1991.

Introduction

On 9 September 1889 John Burns stood on Tower Hill above a massed army of dock workers. Raising his arm in the air and pointing to the coin in his fingers he shouted, 'This, lads, is the Lucknow[1] of Labour, and I myself, looking to the horizon, can see a silver gleam — not of bayonets to be imbued with a brother's blood, but the gleam of the full round orb of the docker's tanner.'

The Great Dock Strike was over, by far the largest strike in Britain since the Chartist mass strike of 1842.[2] For a month it had virtually closed the Thames to river traffic from the City to Tilbury 25 miles down stream. Sixteen thousand pickets had been organised into mobile units provided with food and transport. Daily processions numbering tens of thousands of dock labourers and their supporters had wended their way from the East End through the commercial and financial areas of the City to the West End and Hyde Park collecting donations from bystanders en route.

The stoppage was much more than a *dock* strike. It was a symbol of a massive upsurge of Britain's unskilled workers' drive for liberation from oppression by organisation. But it was also the peak of this drive which had been characterised by a series of smaller, yet significant, struggles. At the end of March 1889 a meeting of labourers in the gas industry took place at Canning Town Public Hall. Their leader, Will Thorne, had beavered away for years winning workers to trade unionism. Eight hundred men joined the union on one night and by mid-April 3,000 had signed up to the newly constituted National Union of Gas Workers and General Labourers. Thorne was assisted in this organisational drive by Karl Marx's youngest daughter, Eleanor. In the autumn of the previous year 5,000 tailors in Leeds had struck forming themselves into a union following their brothers in the Leeds building industry that summer.

Starting this accelerating mass movement were the young women at the Bryant and May match factory in Bow, east London. In July 1888, 1,400 of these women, predominantly under the age of 15 years, struck to secure a wage rise and a cut in the 11½ (winter) and 13½ (summer) hour day. Aided by the well known secularist and socialist Annie Besant, the youngsters collected pennies, handed out leaflets and garnered widespread public sympathy for their cause, which they won, forming the Union of Women Match-makers.

Running parallel with the dock strike in London alone there were at least 40 strikes in other industries from tailoring to food processing, metal working, building, railways and road transport. And strikes continued after the dock strike in London and in most other regions of Britain. They were not confined to the unskilled. Many of the better organised craft sections of industry developed a new militancy gaining members in thousands. The influx was reflected in a massive procession through London on May Day 1890.

Yet the upsurge was to be short lived. A dip in the economy strengthened the hand of an employing class keen for vengeance. Old and new unions were on the rack. Almost all suffered enormous loss of membership. Nevertheless the struggles of the late 80s were not had in vain. Organisation did survive. New Unionism would live to fight other days.

The story of Match Girls, gas workers and dockers has been told many times, rightly celebrating the arrival of unskilled unionism. That they were part of a genuine mass movement involving tens of thousands of working people is less well known. It is the purpose of this book to place them in the wider context and to show how this movement, which might have threatened the stability of late 19th century Britain, was headed off by the conscious efforts of a group of bourgeois apologists aided, perhaps unwittingly, by the newly emerging leadership of the new unions.

The story of the birth of the New Unions is not just of historical interest for they emerged after a very long period of low levels of struggle marked by many defeats. It was a period in which very few people looked to the unskilled to bring about change. They appeared passive with no will to organise and to fight back against the appalling conditions which capitalism had brought them. Yet it was from the ranks of the unskilled that the upsurge came, arguably from one of the most unpromising sections, early teenage females with virtually no history of organised struggle. The Match Girls should give immense heart to workers today who feel helpless in the face of the pressures of capitalism in crisis. If it could happen then, it can happen again.

Those events have another story with ongoing relevance. The impulse and the will to fight undoubtedly came from the energy of the workers themselves. But socialists played a vital part. The new organisations, the Social Democratic Federation (SDF) and the Socialist League, had beavered away for much of the decade in the working class areas addressing the critical issues of the time: unemployment, the eight hour day, starvation wages, criminal working practices as well as wider issues such as free speech and the oppression of the Irish. When the upsurge occurred they were there to help to organise, to arrange collections and to lead. They were limited by their numbers, by their inexperience in situations of industrial upsurge and by their underdeveloped tactics and strategies. Those great events took place before lessons could be learnt from the emergence of the modern trade union bureaucracies, reformist parliamentary parties, the Russian Revolution and the rise of fascism. The same mistakes do not have to be made again.

Part I
The strikes

The Bryant and May Match Girls' strike committee

The Match Girls

On an early July afternoon in 1888 a crowd of 200, mainly teenaged girls, arrived outside a newspaper office in Bouverie Street, off Fleet Street in the City of London. They had come from their factory at Bow in the East End. They had run along the Mile End Road, through Whitechapel and by the Aldgate Pump, along Leadenhall Street near the Stock Exchange and the Bank of England, through crowds of black coated City workers, down Cheapside, through St Paul's Churchyard, up Ludgate Hill and into Fleet Street. Their charge of over two miles was fuelled with outraged anger. They had left their work at the Bryant and May match factory in protest when three of their colleagues had been fired. Management had accused them of telling lies about their working conditions to a left wing journalist, Annie Besant. They had come to her for help.

In the middle and upper class London of the 1880s there was a growing interest in the working and living conditions of the poor of the East End. Polite ladies and gentlemen visited the district to observe, to sympathise, to hand out charity and advice, to report and to agitate and organise. Annie Besant belonged to the reporting, agitating and organising faction. In mid-June in a sitting room in Hampstead a group of socialists had met to discuss pay and working conditions in the sweated trades of the East End. One of their number, Henry Hyde Champion, a member of the Social Democratic Federation, mentioned that Bryant and May, one of the area's biggest employers, had announced monster profits and was one of the major culprits in exploiting its workers.

Annie Besant offered to go down to the factory and find out exactly what the situation was. She stood by the gate till the women came out, persuading a small group to talk to her. Besant returned from the East End with a terrible story of cynical exploitation and disregard for the health and welfare of children and young adults. She had recently founded a weekly agitational paper, *The Link,* in which she wrote up her story of life in the match factory. It was entitled 'White Slavery in London'. She noted that the women suffered an 11½ hour day in winter and a 13½ hour day in summer, standing all the time, apart from a miserly 1½ hour break in total. For this a typical worker earned 4/- a week from which 'splendid salary' she had to eat, clothe and house herself. To add insult her pay was subject to a system of fines: 'If the feet are dirty, or if the ground under the bench is left untidy, a fine of 3d is inflicted, for putting "burnts" — matches that have caught fire during the work on the bench 1s has been forfeited, and one unhappy girl was once fined 2/6 for some unknown crime. If a girl leaves four or five matches on her bench when she goes for a fresh "frame" she is fined 3d, and in some departments a fine of 3d is deducted for talking.'[3]

From the crowd of 200 women at the door, Besant brought a small group into her office where they set up an organising committee. They had a tough task ahead. The sense of injustice had pushed the workers out of the factory and fired their march to town. But, on strike, they would have to face the powerful hostility of the Bryant and May management and there would be over 1,000 mouths to feed. The managing director, Frederick Bryant, was already using his influence on the press. His first statement was widely carried. 'His (sic) employees were liars. Relations with them were very friendly until they had been duped by socialist outsiders. He paid wages above the level of his competitors. He did not use fines. Working conditions were excellent. That deductions from pay had been made to finance the erection of a statue to Mr Gladstone was a preposterous suggestion. He would sue Mrs Besant for libel.'

'Mrs Besant' would not be intimidated. The next issue of *The Link*[4] invited Bryant to sue. Much better, she asserted, to sue her than to sack defenceless poor women. She followed that up with a viciously sarcastic letter to the shareholders:

> You, who are quiet and unobtrusive persons, going about in society as decent respectable folk, honoured as good citizens by your neighbours, nay, some of you looked up

to as guides in religious matters, standing forth as teachers of a divine revelation [she had established that over 50 of the shareholders were ministers of religion], professing to believe in a 'religion of love', and looking down with fine contempt on a poor unbeliever like myself, who tries only to discharge, strenuously and incessantly, the duties which have their root in the common Brotherhood of Man.[5]

With no facilities provided, workers would eat their dinners at their benches. 'They eat disease as seasoning to their bread.' The result was the debilitating and disfiguring phossy jaw. On fines she wrote, 'A system of devilish ingenuity catches them in endless traps and robs them even of part of the poor wages they nominally earn.'

She asked them if they knew:

...that girls are asked to carry boxes on their heads till the hair is rubbed off, and the young heads are bald at 15 years of age? Country clergymen with shares in Bryant and May's, draw down on your knee your 15 year old daughter; pass your hand tenderly over the silky, clustering curls, rejoicing in the dainty beauty of the thick shining tresses. Then like a ghastly vision, let there rise up before you the pale worn face of another man's daughter, with wistful pathetic patient eyes and see her as...she pulls off her battered hat and shows a head robbed of its hair by the constant rubbing of the carried boxes, robbed thereof that your dividends might be larger, Sir Cleric...

She finished by writing, 'I hold you up to the public opprobrium you deserve, and brand you with the shame that is your rightful doom.'[6]

She took a group of 50 workers to parliament. The women catalogued their grievances before a group of MPs, and, afterwards, 'outside the House they linked arms and marched three abreast along the Embankment...' The socialist paper *Justice* reported that, 'A very imposing sight it was too, to see the contrast between these poor 'white slaves' and their opulent sisters'.[7]

Besant's propagandist style was bold and effective and she had a fine eye for the importance of organisation. She addressed the problem of finance. An appeal was launched in *The Link*. Every contribution was listed from the pounds of middle class sympathisers to the pennies of the workers. Large marches and rallies were organised in Regents Park in the West End as well as Victoria Park and Mile End Waste in the east. The strike committee called for support from the London Trades Council. This body, now 25 years old, represented the skilled tradesmen of the capital. It had always behaved exclusively, rejecting contact with the poor and unskilled and cultivating respectability. But the Match Girls' plight even struck at *its* conscience. An appeal was launched and contributions rolled in. One of the Social Democratic Federation activists, Harry Hobart, had participated in strike support work for Lancashire cotton workers the previous year. He had seen how these strongly organised workers operated. He borrowed a hall on Bow Road from a sympathetic gentleman and set up a strike HQ. The strikers were asked to report and sign a register for the allocation of strike pay according to need.

Yet the element the middle classes and especially the employers could not comprehend, was the degree to which these workers could help themselves. They were usually depicted as feckless or tragic victims of their own inadequacies tossed around by market forces. There is no doubt that extreme poverty, often reaching starvation for some, was debilitating, nor that the vagaries of the market could wreak havoc upon individuals and families. But there was also resistance and mutuality. Match workers' open struggles went back at least to 1871. The government had imposed a match tax which threatened jobs. Match workers and the communities from which they came surged out of the East End in a vast march on parliament which ended with a brutal battle with the police in Trafalgar Square and the Embankment:

> A large force of police rushed upon the waiting marchers and snatched away their banners which they threw into the Thames...stones were thrown and police batons swung. All entrances to New Palace Yard were blocked and to escape the fury of the mob, the Chancellor of the Exchequer had to enter the House of Commons by an underground passage.[8]

Then there was the story of the Gladstone Statue. Annie Besant said the girls had told her that the Director, Theodore Bryant, a prominent liberal, had deducted a shilling from their wages as a contribution to the erection of a statue to the Liberal prime minister on Bow Road, near the factory, by the ancient church. Some of the workers had revolted:

> ...many went to the unveiling with stones and bricks in their pockets...later on they surrounded the statue — "we paid for it", they cried savagely — shouting and yelling,

> and a gruesome story is told that some cut their arms and let their blood trickle on the marble, paid for, in truth, by their blood.[9]

The story was told in June 1888 as if it had happened 'the week before'. The statue was actually raised in August of 1882. Given the age, and the turnover of employees, the 1882 participants were probably the mothers and sisters of many of the 1888 workers. But the story of resistance was alive in their collective memory. Short lived strikes had taken place in 1881 and 1886 over wages and conditions but they had been unsuccessful.

Demonstrations and strikes were public events with a powerful capacity to act on memory. There was another serviceable quality to call upon in the struggle: family and community support. Some of the more perceptive commentators had observed this almost with surprise. Poor people looked after each other!

> It was "Ulloa, Tom," and, "Well Bill!" at every platform, a desire to share tobacco, to show kindness and receive favours. These men exist by the generosity of their fellows: and the only good thing that comes of being unemployed is, I help you, and you help me, because we've no place in society.[10]

Another observer noted the 'insolent' confidence of the young women. 'When she leaves the Board School and shakes off home discipline she is like an untrained colt — she resents all attempts to put her into harness...(she) cheeks her employer and laughs at passers by (but) is like wax when a fellow worker falls ill or a collection has to be made for a sick companion. She lends her clothes and her boots...she shares her last crust with a girl out of work...'

The attitude of the writer is certainly patronising. Nevertheless it is clear that the solidarity of the women got through. She noted that, when money was being paid out on Mile End Waste, 'few people could fail to be touched by the way in which the girls were determined to stand together at all costs. 'I can pawn this for you', 'I'll lend you that', in every direction girls might be seen plotting how they could help one another on until Bryant and May gave them back their pennies'.[11]

Apparently hidden from the view of most historians[12] is the fact that the Match Girls were largely Irish or of Irish origin, though a director interviewed in 1893 for the *Girls' Own Paper,* noted 'that all our hands, men and women, hail from the Emerald Isle by birth or lineage'.[13] This may have added an important ingredient to their mutuality and maybe even to their readiness to fight at that time. It was well known and recorded that communities of Irish immigrants shared a strong identity and were ready to defend it fiercely. Charles Booth in his monumental survey of east London pointed to a particular area as being noted for sending more police to hospital than any other block in London. Known as the Fenian Barracks, its men would not allow one of their number to be taken and would keep out 'invaders' with barricades.[14] At least 23 match workers lived in the 'Fenian Barracks', five in Fern Street adjoining them and another 24 in Sophia Street and Rook Street, Poplar — all predominantly 'Irish' Streets according to the 1891 Census.[15] The Strike Register compiled by the strike committee lists over

600 workers by name and address. Large numbers have obviously Irish names.[16] So the workers were Irish and they largely lived in close proximity to each other. The Irish had also built a network of cultural, religious and political organisations keeping identity and contact alive.

It is also the case that the 1880s were a decade in which Irish affairs were extremely high profile. From famine, to evictions, to coercion, to terrorism, to Land Reform and to Home Rule, Irish matters were never far from the top of the news agenda. The Irish in Britain were continuously engaged with these issues, nowhere more prominently than in London. Mass demonstrations were almost a commonplace. Tens of thousands of the London Irish participated and it is extremely likely that the communities which housed the Match Girls had played their part.

There was sometimes a show of affection and support for Gladstone for some of his Irish policies. At the time of the unveiling of the statue in 1882, referred to above, the government's Irish Land Reform promises were a hot issue, though coercion was also on the agenda after the murder of the new Chief Secretary to Ireland in Phoenix Park, Dublin, in May. Lord Carlingford, a former Cabinet colleague of Gladstone gave the address in which he made special and prolonged reference to the 'great' man's sympathy for, and commitment to, the people of Ireland. The local paper reported that, 'It was as if the whole of the East End had turned out to witness the ceremony'.[17] Gladstone's apparent popularity on the street in no way diminishes the possibility of there having been sharp antagonism among Bryant's employees to the behaviour of their Liberal employer.

Then there is John Denvir's account of Hyde Park demonstrations:

> Indeed the Irish may be seen to be the backbone of...popular movements in London... Not only do you find them in the ranks of the purely Catholic and Irish societies, with their bands, banners, and patriotic emblems, but in connection with other political and temperance organisations — if one may judge from the handsome banners, on which you often see depicted such subjects as "Sarsfield," "The Irish Parliament house," and "O'Connell'; with quotations from Tom Moore and harps and shamrocks galore.[18]

Finally just three months before the strike a mass demonstration took place on Tower Hill, so near to Limehouse, Poplar and Bow. The issue was the imprisonment of three Nationalists:

> There was to be witnessed...procession after procession, marching from every street and road emerging onto the hill, their banners flying gaily and their bands playing... Green was without doubt the favourite colour of the day... Green banners waved lazily in the breeze borne from the Thames; green sashes relieved the monotony of black coats; green ribbons dangled from button holes and encircled hats; and green plumes waved from hats and hands... The speeches at all the platforms were vigorous and earnest; but those of the two East End Irish delegates were received with special enthusiasm, dealing as they did with their recent experiences in Ireland.[19]

It is very likely that some of the future strikers and their families were present. The excitement that spring and summer may have been a force waiting to explode. That its probable Irish dimension was displaced into a struggle over wages and conditions at work does not diminish its force as a possible ingredient in that struggle as it may also have been 12 months later in the August of 1889.

The Match Girls stayed out for three weeks. The London Trades Council, at the strike committee's invitation, interceded. George Shipton, its secretary, met Frederick Bryant and set up a meeting between him and a group of strikers. The young women had to face humiliation while Bryant cross-examined them, tricking them into giving answers which suited his particular view of events. Predictably perhaps, Shipton concurred with him in diminishing the force of the workers' grievances and sought to help him to effect a public face-saving compromise which gave the strikers very little but did enable them to establish a trade union, the very first in the new movement for the unionisation of the unskilled.[20] This in itself was no mean achievement.

Bryant's arrogance was underlined six months later when he gave a supercilious and self justificatory account of the strike to the annual meeting of shareholders. That Bryant was badly shaken by the events is testified by consulting his private correspondence.[21] Unfortunately for the Match Girls of 1888, it only became available in the 1980s when the company records were deposited in Hackney Archives after a company merger closed down the Fairfield Road site.

But there is a nice postscript. The Match Girls deservedly became heroines of the labour movement. They would probably be delighted to know that they continued to rattle the Bryant and May management right up to the time of closure. For documentation of this we have to thank an obsessive managing director and his company secretary. They collected for over 50 years, from all over the world, the tiniest fragments of information about the Match Girls and their strike. Their files contain numerous letters from schoolchildren and their teachers asking for help in projects on the strike. Every single one assumes the workers were right.

Funniest of all though is the file on dramas. There have been at least three attempts to put the story onto the stage. The writers and directors each approached the firm for information and help. The correspondence indicates the continuing sensitivity and self justification motivating the management. When *The Match Girls* was heading for the West End in 1963, behind the scenes the company tried to block its production whilst appearing to give a positive response to the requests. They approached Jack Hylton Enterprises seeking cuts, 'by removing all references to Bryant and May from the script'. They employed lawyers and PR firms. The lawyer advised no action. The PR firm suggested 'killing it with kindness', 'Exploit it — by this we mean the use of such extravagant gimmicks as buying out the whole theatre for the first night and taking all the Fairfield employees to it.' The PR letter ended with the advice to 'your advertising agents...to have deleted the word "strike" from all your advertising, unless they can give it a particular deliberate twist!'[22]

The Match Girls have had an astonishing power to speak to us over the last century. The meeting at the factory gate that June, of the socialist activist and the group of angry young working class women, was a key moment in the birth of a vast social movement which would be celebrated in labour and socialist history as the New Unionism. Annie Besant was quickly involved in disputes involving match workers at Paces in Bromley-by-Bow, a Bryant and May company, with more match workers in Aberdeen, tin box makers in south London, and the chain-makers of Cradley Heath.[23] In October a new union on the docks entered its first struggle. This was the Tea Operatives and General Labourer's Association which struck at Tilbury for 1d an hour. Ben Tillett, its leader, said in his autobiography, 'We put the wind up the Tilbury Dock management,' and paid tribute to the Match Girls whose strike he called 'the beginning of the social convulsion which produced the "New" Unionism'.[24]

But the strike is not just of historic interest. It is an absolutely critical example of how after decades of low struggle and disappointment a militant movement can revive. Its genesis could come from the most unpredictable and apparently unpromising source. Call centre personnel? Supermarket till staff? Well, not in 1888! It was 12 to 15 year old kids in the match industry!

From Match Girls to dock strike

THE EPICENTRE OF ACTIVITY in the mass movement of 1889 was London. Though there were strikes in most industrial areas of Britain in that year and the years which immediately followed, it was in the East End that the movement peaked and it was events in the East End which ultimately determined the fate of that movement. The Match Girls' struggle of summer 1888 was the touch paper which lit the fuse that was to run right up to September 1889 with John Burns's famous speech on Tower Hill at the end of the Great Dock Strike.

It is easy to see how those women provided the inspiration. They were young. They were loud. They were confident. They charged about the area holding meetings and parades. They forced the Bryant and May bosses to climb down. And they won! They were the children, the sisters, the cousins and the friends of the strikers of '89, the carters, rope workers, flour millers, iron foundry workers, hod carriers, printers' labourers, jam, cake and sweet makers, railway labourers, tailors, laundresses, gas stokers and dock labourers. They lived in the same streets in Canning Town, Poplar, Limehouse, Wapping, and Bromley and Bow. They'd gone to the same schools, went to the same churches, visited the same pubs, joined the same social clubs, laughed and cried together at the same baptisms, weddings and wakes.[25]

The records don't tell us much about the winter of 1888-89 but when the spring came and people were out on the streets again (often as an escape from damp, overcrowded homes) it was the gas stokers who were first into the fray. In that winter the Beckton Gas Works employers had introduced the 'iron man', a machine for charging the retorts with coal and drawing off the coke. Will Thorne, who was to become leader of the new union, wrote:

> The machines made the work heavier for the men. In fact so hard and rapid was the work that we often had no time to eat our food between the charges. The machine was constantly breaking down, and this would put us behind with the work, for, breakdown or no, we had to do the same number of charges...we had a heart-breaking task.[26]

Thorne had come from Birmingham where he had been fired for militancy in 1881. He said, 'I talked to my companions about my previous experience and told them that the task allotted to us was more than we could do.' He spoke to the management on behalf of the men but got nowhere. He could only win a few for strike action. He campaigned, quietly at first, for a week's holiday and for the eight hour day. He also says he was a model workman giving the bosses no obvious excuse for dismissal.

Then on 31 March 1889 he and others convened a meeting at Canning Town Public Hall. The docker Ben Tillett was on the platform with some comrades from the SDF including a compositor, Harry Hobart. The National Union of Gas Workers and General Labourers was formed. Eight hundred men joined that day, dropping their first subscription into pails. On subsequent Sundays they formed contingents which toured gas works and other workplaces. In two weeks over 3,000 workers had joined.

The new union petitioned the employers for an eight hour day. 'Shorten the hours and prolong your lives' was Thorne's slogan. A month later most of the gas company employers in the area, including Beckton, had agreed to meet the demand—with only the threat of strike action. In his autobiography Thorne wrote:

> The formation of our union was the definite establishment, and the beginning of what has been termed "New Unionism". It was the culmination of long years of socialist propaganda amongst the underpaid and oppressed workers. Politics had been preached to them, vague indefinite appeals to revolution, but we offered them something tangible, a definite, clearly lighted road out of their misery, a trade union that would improve their wages and conditions; that would protect them from the petty tyranny of employers... They came in thousands, within six months we had made over 20,000 members in different parts of the country. We showed the way to the dockers and other unskilled workers; our example and our success gave them hope. Within a short time the "New Unionism" was in full flower.[27]

He fails to give credit to the Match Girls. Nevertheless, in terms of a breakthrough to mass trade unionism Thorne was undoubtedly right. The impact of the gas workers' success must have been considerable in the East End alone. As we shall see, there was a veritable rash of strikes that summer but the biggest and most significant was certainly the dock strike which broke out in the middle of August. It was a strike on an altogether different scale from the previous ones. There were over 150,000 workers on the Thames riverside. A strike could have significance for the whole economy.

In the late 19th century the Port of London was the biggest and wealthiest port in the world. It was at the hub of the world's most powerful trading empire handling a vast traffic in commodities amongst which the most substantial were tea, sugar, grain, bonded items, coal, timber and a multitude of finished goods. The port consisted of ten large docks, constructed in the previous 80 years on a piecemeal basis, and innumerable river wharves. Although by 1889 mergers had concentrated ownership of docking facilities, there was no central authority and Thames commerce was characterised by fierce competition between both dock and wharf owners with a strong tendency to specialise in the handling of specific goods subject to seasonality, and tidal and weather conditions.

The challenge offered by steam and other developments in technology had been met by the construction of new deep water facilities down river rather than by the modernisation of existing ones. The result was a port dispersed over nearly 30 miles of river with rising land transport costs.

Problems were intensified by the creeping obsolescence of older facilities and compounded by shipping companies' preference for linking their loading and unloading to riverside wharves served by lighter traffic to avoid docking charges. Except at the absolute peaks of economic boom there was a surfeit of facilities and a constant pressure on profit margins.

In part the port labour force reflected the character of this economic structure. It was large: over 150,000 workers and their families depended upon port work for their livelihood. It was largely casual, perhaps no more than 10 percent having permanent and regular employment. Characteristically, men huddled *en masse* outside the dock gates or at the wharves throughout the day, waiting for the call to work. Approached by the 'caller on' or 'sweater', men struggled to get the ticket:

> Coats, flesh, and even ears were torn off... The strong literally threw themselves over the heads of their fellows and battled...through the kicking, punching, cursing crowds to the rails of the 'cage' which held them like rats — mad human rats who saw food in the ticket.[28]

It was a highly fragmented labour force. Workers lived in local communities round specific dockyards and wharves relating to specific employers and cargoes. There was little mobility between docks, producing, over the whole port area, an enormous surplus of labour. Its fragmented nature had not been much affected by the expansion and relocation of facilities in the century's last quarter. So much depended upon being noticed in the crowd at the dock gate that workers were loath to try their luck elsewhere where they were not known at all. But also employer separation and discrete geographical location meant that there were few means of communicating short term work opportunities from one locality to another.

There was another major source of division: a complex sense of hierarchy attached to particular occupations. The primary division was between 'on board' work and 'on land' work, the latter further nuanced between the waterside and the warehouse. The former carried the highest status usually reflected in higher pay, but even there, the stowing of cargo carried greater kudos than its unloading, and working on ocean going ships was superior to coastal vessel work. Even deck work and hold work carried different status.

The lightermen who operated the small craft plying between large ship and shore were at the summit of pay and status. The more numerous elite group were the stevedores loading ocean going craft, who claimed status deriving from their responsibility for the security of men and cargoes. Training and practice in cargo handling gave them skills difficult to reproduce quickly. This acted as some kind of defence against summary dismissal and replacement. It was reflected in their relative success in union organisation, though they remained vulnerable to the vagaries of the market, the tides and weather and technical change.

A further 'fault line' running across work in the port was produced by the system of employers 'subcontracting' to work gangs in some facilities. Most notorious were the London Docks where the worker had to buy his job in the pub. Subcontract encouraged an impetus towards small group discipline, privacy over sums earned, cheating, favouritism and exclusivity.

Apart from the growing predominance of steamships with their greater size and use in all weathers, new technologies were slow to reach cargo handling. Hard physical labour, used in appropriate fashion, was still the most necessary quality in its workers. So it was taxing and potentially dangerous to the workers' health. Serious and sometimes fatal injuries from falls, loose cargo and carelessly slung winches and moving gantries were very common. Long term deterioration and disability from the unprotected handling of cargo such as coal and corn with their permanent clouds of dust and constant outside work in inclement weather curtailed the dock workers' productive lives. Such factors conspired to make it a young man's occupation. Older men were shuffled off into more and more marginal areas of work accompanied by abject poverty and the begging bowl.

An over-supplied labour market demanded constant, if episodic, replenishment by young fit men. The first source of recruitment came from dock work families where such activity might go back several generations. But there had been an enormous growth of port facilities during the 19th century. Its demands could not be met from the indigenous riverside population. The paucity and irregularity of earnings were not inviting to the healthiest and most vigorous sections of the population anyway, especially in periods of general economic expansion.

Typically in such situations, the industry turned to migrants from Ireland and from the countryside. Both groups were welcomed by employers. The bulk of such workers usually arrived fit, enthusiastic, unencumbered by any collectivist tradition and ready to work at any wages on offer. Poverty was relative and at least in the booms some income from riverside work was superior to the starvation experienced by those left behind on the land in Ireland. And life for the rural labourer in England was hardly much better in a period of severe agricultural decline. Recruitment of new workers was predominantly Irish with the exceptions of the new docks at Tilbury in rural Essex and in the Surrey Commercial Docks which both drew in substantial numbers of displaced English farm labourers. The high incidence of Irish Catholic workers was a powerful force in the strike starting at all, the rapidity of its spread and probably for the means of its settlement.

This complex situation had placed the balance of forces firmly with the employers during the past century. These men could regard their employees with considerable contempt as, in the parlance of that time, 'dock rats'. Unlike certain other groups — engineers, textile operatives, and even coal miners — dock workers had gained little benefit from the expansion of the Victorian economy from mid-century. Wages and working conditions had not improved. The standard wage rate had remained at 5d per hour for two decades though modest improvements in living standards may have accrued from the fall of commodity prices in the Great Depression.

However, the wages problem derived only partly from the lowness of the basic rate, though this was a genuine enough grievance. Much more pertinent were the irregularity of earnings produced by hourly, daily, weekly and seasonal idleness, the lack of clarity over what constituted overtime and the complex calculations of bonus payments or, as they were called in this industry, 'plus'.

The wholehearted enthusiasm of thousands of dockers, their families and communities when the strike broke out in the summer of '89, is suggestive of a massive collective release from oppression. A system surviving for so long in a series of finely graded sub-systems of hierarchy accumulates a mass of individual and group grievances which are largely repressed or diverted. They are repressed in the public space at work in front of the employer and his agents because not to do so would lead to the docking of wages, dismissal and possibly the courts and prison. They might be diverted into minor acts of sabotage, pilfering and humorous or satirical representations of the boss and the foreman in relationships with workmates. Beyond the working environment frustration might be taken out in street fighting, assaults upon girlfriends, wives and children and leisure activities like bare knuckle boxing, dog and cock fights.

There was a whole intermittent history of 'walk-offs' and, no doubt, many more were just not recorded. Until the Great Strike there had only been one large and sustained attempt at trade union organisation. This had occurred in the short lived boom which preceded the onset of the Great Depression in 1873. It was the conflict in which Thames stevedore trade unionism was born and out of which it survived organisationally, despite sustained recession over a decade. Central to the success of this endeavour had been socialist and radical activists from outside the industry including a member of the General Council of the First International.

It might be argued, therefore, that there were both informal and formal forces at work over a considerable period of time which would make an outbreak of conflict likely — at some point. In a capitalist society it is inescapably true that workers obtain only a small portion of the wealth which they create. This exploitative relationship may be experienced more or less severely in given workplaces. The particular conditions of work in the ports — low wages, endemic irregularity of employment and contemptuous management — created one of the very worst situations for workers in Britain.

The late 1880s were a time when there was a coalescence of elements which could lead to action. In addition to the Match Girls and gas workers the new seamen's union was engaged in a highly successful membership drive. The incidence of Irish workers in docks and community at a moment of intense feeling and activity on the Irish issue could have proved a catalyst. And the tiny strand of socialist democracy running back through the struggles for parliamentary reform to the Chartists was present and active in the East End. One socialist activist, the dock worker Ben Tillett, had assisted both Match Girls and gas workers. He had already launched a union drive among the tea operatives in 1887 and was a regular speaker at dock gate meetings up and down the riverside — as far off as Tilbury. The possibility of collective action was at least part of dock worker consciousness. Faced with overcapacity and bankruptcy the employers were flexing their muscles for a further war of attrition upon dockers' meagre living standards. The employers at the new Tilbury dock, opened only in

1886, used the rawness of their new labour force to offer only 4d per hour. All dockers were being severely pressed.

The catalyst was the 'plus' system. Plus was a payment above the hourly rate based on tonnage moved on a shift. A kind of piece work, it could have been remunerative if the workers had known the basis on which it was calculated. In the employers' hands it was a ready means of reducing the wages bill. Workers were rightly suspicious. A dispute on board ship, *The Lady Armstrong,* in the South West India Dock, in August, was the effective issue on which action started to roll.

An early squabble between rivals for the leadership was resolved after a mass meeting at the South Dock on 12 August. Ben Tillett's organisation assumed the leadership, forming branches throughout the dock area and growing in a matter of weeks to 18,000 members. Tillett immediately involved Tom McCarthy of the stevedores and Tom Mann and John Burns, both activists in the Social Democratic Federation.

The strike began on 14 August and was initially aimed at the piece work systems of the West India Dock Company. However, Tillett soon formulated a more comprehensive set of demands:

- Abolition of plus and contract systems
- Minimum half day period of employment
- Taking on times to be reduced to two per day
- Overtime to be penalised by raising the rate of difference from one to two pennies per hour
- Basic hourly rate to be raised to 6d

The divisions among dock employees meant that there were different pressures operating on different groups and there was no guarantee that others would follow the lead of Tillett and the West India Dock men. The critical group was the stevedores because their work affected everyone round them and they were already the best organised group on the Thames. However, the strike's main issue did not affect them at all. Their leader, Tom McCarthy, was a strong advocate of action, but initially, as an individual. The employers made an early and critical error of judgement. They immediately moved blackleg labour into an area where stevedores would have to work alongside them. This the stevedores refused to do and three days into the strike they too joined.

On the following day meetings at the huge Victoria and Albert Docks resolved to join in and London, St Katherine's, Millwall and Tilbury followed within the week. At the end of the week the lightermen came out and so too did the corn porters of the south side plus sundry other riverside workers: sailors, warehousemen and wharfmen. By 22 August the Port of London was at an almost complete standstill.

Nevertheless, the strike remained precarious. The employers, grouped together in the face of the enemy, were slow to understand the unfolding situation. Their first instinct was to rely on their stereotype of the dockers as feckless incompetents. Their Joint Committee did not respond to the strike committee's letter of demands. Towards the end of August there was some wavering among the strikers with groups returning to work to be pulled out again by pickets. This was especially true of the south side of the Thames where grievances did not wholly correspond with those of the north side.

There were also serious financial problems. The strikers relied entirely upon donations from unions, individual workers, charities, churches and sympathetic members of the public. Impressive though donations were, they could not meet the rapidly mounting costs of feeding perhaps 50,000 dockers and their families. On 29/30 August the strike committee tried to escalate the dispute by calling for a general strike across London in support of the dockers. It was a risky proposition. After a couple of days of panicky discussion it was revoked. Historians have tended to dismiss the call as a panic move of desperate men, yet the circumstances demand discussion.[29]

In the middle of the last week in August attempts were made to picket out the south side of the river. Many of those dock workers already received more than the modest demands made by the strike committee, but fortunately for the strike there were local grievances to work upon. Tom Mann was sent there to liaise and to organise picketing. Another socialist, Harry Quelch of the SDF, was struggling to bring together a general union, the South Side Labour Protection League, with its centre in Bermondsey. The solidarity of the south side workers was, in industrial terms, the fillip the strike needed. Almost as significant was the news that Australian dockers and other trade unionists were responding to the London men's financial appeal and the figure of £30,000 sent from Australia was decisive in giving the strike's leaders the leverage to maintain pressure on the employers.

The dispute was taken to the general public through daily mass marches through the City which made an enormous impact upon middle class conscience. Two young civil servants, H Llewellyn Smith and Vaughan Nash, left an impressive account:

> The eastern circle of the City...was clogged with the procession, which, emerging into Aldgate, going eastwards, hardly escaped being involved with the passing tide. The citizens of London will not forget it soon...when fifty thousand men trudged moodily past shop and office and warehouse... First came a posse of police, behind whom the marshals of the procession, with axes and scarfs, reserved a clear space for the leaders... Next came the brass band of the stevedores, following which streamed the multitude whose calling lay at the docks and riverside. Such finery as they boasted in the way of flags and banners had been lent by friendly and trade societies...there were burly stevedores, lightermen, ship painters, sailors and firemen riggers, scrapers, engineers, shipwrights, permanent men got up respectably, preferably cleaned up to look like permanents, and unmistakable casuals with vari-coloured patches on their faded greenish garments; Foresters and Sons of the Phoenix in gaudy scarfs; Doggett's prize winners, a stalwart battalion of watermen marching proudly in long scarlet coats, pink stockings and velvet caps with huge pewter badges on their breasts, like decorated amphibian huntsmen; coalies in wagons flashing aggressively for coppers with bags tied to the end of poles, a brother coalie in effigy attached as

figure head to one of their vehicles, placarded with the announcement that he wouldn't go a step higher up the ladder on which he sprawled till the docker got his tanner; skiffs mounted on wheels manned by stalwart watermen; ballast heavers laboriously winding and tipping an empty basket, Father Neptune on his ear in tinsel crown and flowing locks, surrounded by his suite, — Brittania in a Union Jack skirt, the doctor in a faultless hat, and the barber brandishing a huge razor ready for the victims of the Equator on the other side of the car. Emblems quaint and pathetic were carried in the ranks, the docker's cat and the sweater's cat, the docker's dinner and the sweater's dinner, the docker's baby and the sweater's baby, diminutive and ample, respectively; Sir Hardwood (a gentleman understood to be connected with the Joint Committee), attired in mortar board, gown and mask, gravely saluted the bystanders and bowed low in front of the Dock House. The bass dressers, locked out for forming a union, brought up the rear, carrying their bass brooms like lictors.

Such was the strike procession. It had its moods—was merry on some days, taciturn on others, laughed at the Dock House sometimes, howled at it at others, but it never lost command over itself or caused serious anxiety to its leaders or to the citizens of London.[30]

It is difficult to know the degree of anxiety 'in the citizens of London', but there was evidence of the movement spreading as 'numberless trades threw in their lot with the strikers, abandoned their work and joined the processions'.[31] Fearing further escalation and the growing influence of the socialists in the leadership, a committee of 'wise men' was established to negotiate with the employers ostensibly on behalf of the workers. Led by the head of the Roman Catholic Church in England, Cardinal Henry Manning, this committee entered into discussions with the port employers in early September. It was by no means an easy negotiation, for the port directors had a clear agenda. Norwood, the employers' spokesman, said that concessions 'will absolutely spoil the game we are playing...which we are not playing for our own hands...but for the ship-owners, for the manufacturers, and for the entire industries, I might say, of the East End.'[32] However, there was pressure on the proprietors from within their own ranks and from their customers the ship owners.

After a few days the 'wise men' brought a settlement to the strike committee which, after some indecision, and in the face of Manning's irritation, it turned down. The settlement achieved most of the men's demands on paper, but as a sop to the employers' pride, the date for enacting it was to be postponed till January 1890. This was the point the leaders found unacceptable. Manning gracelessly took it back to the employers and finally obtained a settlement with only a one month delay. The leaders then took it up enthusiastically and the strike was brought to an end on 14 September. A mass rally took place in Hyde Park on the next day following a vast march from the East End. The victory was heralded throughout working class circles as a triumph: the effective launching of trade unionism for the unskilled in Britain.

The success of the strike had depended upon a number

of key operations involving picketing, the raising and distribution of subsistence for the strikers and the maintenance of a high public profile involving non-dock workers. These activities were organised by a vigorous group of leaders consisting of Ben Tillett, Tom Mann, Tom McCarthy, John Burns and Harry Orbell, another dock worker activist.

Tillett had long understood the vital function of effective picketing. During his exhausting attempts to deal with the Tilbury employers in 1888 he had ruminated on the problem of matching the tiny resources of his new union to the giant task in hand. He needed a 'colossal picketing system'. He saw 'how the Thames might and could be made idle...a thousand million pounds of financial power brought to a standstill. These were my dreams. My terrible dreams.'[33] It is estimated that the strike committee mobilised some 16,000 pickets during the strike, a phenomenal achievement considering that Tillett's union had less than 800 members on the strike's first day. And of course there were countless gates, wharves and railway stations and sidings to be covered.

The employers lost no time in attempting to recruit blacklegs, sparing no cost to bring them from far afield including Belgium. They even resorted to disguising them in bowler hats, dark suits and umbrellas. When discovered, the tactic was commemorated in effigy by the dockers. In the first few days Mann and Burns operated a flying picket, approaching dock gates and walls and calling men out as they travelled—with great success. Tillett and Orbell travelled the 20 miles to Tilbury bringing out the Tilbury men where Orbell stayed to organise daily picketing. A correspondent from a Newcastle newspaper travelled with flying pickets in north east London. He really captured the excitement:

> A body of strikers assembled at Radcliffe in the East End and proceeded on foot and in vans over a pre-arranged route embracing the north east, the north and north west districts of London, meetings being held in each of the districts and speeches delivered urging the labouring portion of the population to aid the dock labourers in their demand for better wages. At King's Cross which is admitted to be the largest coal centre in London the leaders of the movement made speeches which had the desired effect upon the coal porters and car men who at once agreed to the request that that they should strike for advance of a penny per ton. Unanimous. They then proceeded to the Great Eastern goods depot, Messrs E James and Co at Devonshire Street, which employs 3-4000 coal workers (success), Midland Railway, Camden coal depot at Chalk Farm (failed), derrick men and car drivers followed...men were leaving work in thousands.[34]

The organisation was superb despite extreme financial privation. Harry Orbell, a strike committee member, deployed numerous loyal activists to work alongside blacklegs giving the strike committee a useful flow of information. Since many of the blacklegs were kept in ignorance of the strike's course, or even its objectives, such activity was invaluable and pickets gave a good deal of attention to debating with them as well as abusing them. In several cases this led to blacklegs withdrawing their labour and joining the strike. Others returned to their home towns by 'assisted passage'.

Tom Mann was especially effective on the south side of the river when the workers there 'wobbled' in the first week in September due to an apparent agreement by their employers to the terms of their demands. He increased the number of pickets and reorganised them working with phenomenal energy, 'a streak of human quicksilver, here, there and everywhere, commanding, pleading, cajoling, enthusing'.[35]

The pickets had to be fed, as did the mass of striking dock workers and their families, and this was the strike leadership's biggest headache. Very few dock workers earned enough to save. At best, even when working, they eked out an existence at about subsistence level. So they plunged into strike action with no resources. With less than 1,000 members, and only a couple of years of existence, Tillett's union was virtually penniless. The strike could only survive from donations. Part of the rationale for holding daily marches throughout the City was to keep up morale among the strikers but an important by-product was the daily donations given by bystanders. A measure of the impact of this strike is the amount of money which, according to Smith and Nash, came from black coated City workers as the procession passed.[36]

A number of the craft unions in the TUC gave modest donations but that body itself was hardly helpful at all. Some charity organisations and churches organised soup kitchens. The meagre funds coming to the strike committee had to be handled with great care. The distribution point was Wroot's Coffee House in Poplar, the headquarters of Tillett's fledgling union. It was regularly besieged by famished people, not all of whom were striking dockers. Naturally news of handouts was a magnet for the vast impoverished masses of the East End. Qualification for a 'ticket' very quickly became a union card and soon there were more than 20,000 new members in Tillett's union. The actual handouts were controlled by Tom Mann personally:

> There was a crowd of nearly 4,000 men waiting outside. Mann pledged them his word that every man should get his ticket if he would take his turn and bide his time; then planting himself in the doorway, his back jammed against one side of the frame, his foot up against the other, he allowed the men to creep in, one at a time, under his leg. Hour after hour went by, while Tom Mann stripped to the waist, stuck to his post, forcing the men down as they came up to him, chaffing, persuading, remonstrating, whenever the swaying mass of dockers got out of control, until at last the street was cleared.[37]

Soon the distribution of benefit was localised but until the arrival of the Australian donation the strikers remained vulnerable to starvation. The leaders had to practise extreme vigilance and it is great credit to them that it did hold together long enough to achieve a favourable settlement. The energy, determination and organisational skill of Ben Tillett, the physical strength and tactical sense of Tom Mann and the rhetorical power, flamboyance and daring of John Burns were a formidable combination, perhaps the most powerful in the whole of British labour history.

Nevertheless they had neither the will nor apparently the inclination to broaden their demands, nor were the strike's occurrence and scale seen as a vehicle with political possibilities. The vague, though important, objective of establishing general unionism was of course there, but there is little sense of a class struggle directed more broadly at targets other than the intransigent dock employers. It is clear that the bosses were an obdurate bunch and a fitting target of dockers' anger. Their post-strike behaviour is testimony to that. They dragged their feet on implementation of the agreement and carried on a public denigration of the strikers' tactics—even criticising the Metropolitan Police for failing to uphold the law on picketing. But in a strange sort of mirroring, strike leaders praised the police for their moderation, failing to draw attention to this 'moderation' as a direct consequence of the authorities' understanding of the strikers' potent mass power. The most slavish in his attitude to the police was Burns, himself a victim of their 'moderation' in Hyde Park three years earlier! Perhaps there was an irony in his victory speech lost in transcription, though his transition to Liberal MP and cabinet minister in the next two decades makes this somewhat doubtful.

It may well be the demonstration of disciplined mass power that best explains the relatively uncritical response of the British establishment to the events of 1889. To have distinguished members of the ruling class siding with strikers is a rare enough event in the political calendar. For them to be siding with a section of society historically abused and held in contempt, though feared, is even more remarkable. It needs explanation.

The poor of the East End had been the subject of several social inquiries and reports in the past decade. The poor, or the 'residuum', as it was described, had been the subject of middle and upper class fear and loathing for much of the century since capitalism had triggered the headlong rush from the land into the towns and cities. Usually seen as the creators rather than the victims of poverty and disease, the new city dwellers were felt as a noxious, drunken, riotous and threatening presence which uncontrolled might sweep 'civilisation' away.

A sigh of relief was breathed when the extension of the franchise in 1867 had not brought about the disintegration of society as its rulers knew it. The government had hastened to domesticate the new electorate of largely skilled workers by the introduction of state education, and sections of the middle classes encouraged and promoted temperance and organised leisure activities. Of course, none of this dealt with poverty or the large pools of humanity concentrated in the margins of industrial and commercial society. However, there were optimists in the ruling cliques who believed that extending the franchise once more, to include most males, would have similar 'civilising' effects to the previous one.

Nevertheless it was felt that more should be known about the 'co-electors'. From the 60s the paternalist conscience of the middle class had conducted missionary expeditions into London's East End. By 1887 there were some 100 such agencies. Incidentally, one surveyed the 'electorate' and discovered that in Poplar, Stepney and Hackney, less than 20 percent of adult males were eligible to vote even after the advance of 1884!

It had become fashionable for middle and upper class ladies to have a period of 'slumming' in the East End as part of their education. Some of them actually managed to do useful investigative work which did not simply patronise the local population. The first serious survey was conducted by a Congregationalist minister, Andrew Mearns, concerned by the impact of 'the demon drink', but shaken by the evidence of general dereliction due to poverty. His pamphlet, *The Bitter Cry of Outcast London,* was published in 1883 creating a considerable stir on the eve of the Third Reform Bill. In 1886 Charles Booth had commenced his massive inquiry, *London Life and Labour,* which was to expose, in serial form, the appalling situation to middle and upper class readers.

As we have seen, it was not only religiously motivated sentiment that took the middle classes among the poor. The 1880s were also the decade which saw the revival of socialist analysis and the green shoots of New Unionism. The socialists took up the scandal of unemployment. One manifestation was the belching into the West End of the East End's poor in 1886 and 1887 which had ended in rioting and looting. Some of the upper classes subsided into helpless panic, but others saw that there was a degree of inevitability in the development of an organised voice for the rabble. The key question for them was who would give the lead.

Most prominent amongst this kind of thinking was Cardinal Henry Manning, the senior papal representative in Great Britain. An upper class convert to Catholicism, he was the son of a Governor of the Bank of England and the brother of a former dock proprietor. Although an arch-conservative on issues of doctrine, Manning was unquestionably moved by the poverty and desperation of the London poor. He had aligned himself with radicals and reforming movements from the 1850s onwards and was strongly supportive of moderate social reform. But he also saw in the despair of the poor a potential for a violent settling of accounts with the social system, an awareness sharpened by the increased street activity of the mid-80s. In an article written just after the dock strike ended he referred to 'the fear which haunted him that at any moment some fool or madman might step in and wreck all the efforts of the leaders to maintain order'.[38] Managing the inevitable drive to social and political consciousness of the masses was his quest. He was thought to be a strong influence behind Pope Leo XIII's famous encyclical *Rerum Novarum* of 1891 which, whilst sanctioning trade unionism and even strikes, condemned socialism. This was major shift in Catholic teaching and one which recognised the growing potential power of the working class on an international scale.

Manning set out to befriend and 'advise' the emerging working class leaders. He had some success too. Ben Tillett wrote of him 'as one of the master forces of my life at this period'.[39] Even Tom Mann was captivated. In his *Memoirs* he wrote, 'I have before commented upon his wonderful features, and upon the ultra refined manner that always characterised him. He was perfectly natural, and simple, and I was entirely at ease with him'.[40]

It is a token of the immaturity of the movement at the time that apparently none of the strike leaders questioned the advisability of using intermediaries to settle the strike. This is not a comment on the energy, determination and courage of these men. As militant representatives of their class they were exemplary, sharing the privation of the rank and file and engaged on the ground at every stage. But it is significant that the delegation meeting the employers consisted of a Cardinal, a Bishop, a former Lord Mayor of London, a captain of industry, two bankers and a Liberal MP. Even though the three most prominent leaders of the strike were socialists and members of the SDF they clearly lacked the political confidence to represent the dockers' position themselves.

So the triumph of the dockers must be qualified by a recognition that a transforming moment for the labour movement in Britain carried within it an important pointer to the movement's future direction. This was the acceptance of a leadership embodying the values and objectives of the ruling class, a factor all too prevalent in the launching of the ILP in the next decade.

It will be recalled that Burns and Mann were not dockers themselves, a further token of the movement's weakness at the start of the strike. Yet the nature of the leadership speaks of a fluidity in the situation. The running of the strike and indeed the nature of its ending were free from the dead hand of bureaucracy. If the ending was unsatisfactory it was also the case that its running was open to the involvement of committed and enthusiastic outsiders. These were people who had played a key role in the Bryant and May, gas workers' and other initiatives of the previous year. And, stretching back just a little further, members of the SDF and Socialist League had been very active among the miners of Northumberland with no apparent hostility being shown by union officials.

However, the dockers' strike was a triumph. It transformed the image of the poor and unskilled from a feckless rabble into a class capable of being organised into trade unions. This process had started with the activity of the women at Bryant and May, the gas workers, the seafarers and the port workers in Hull, Glasgow and Liverpool. It was enhanced enormously by the dockers' victory and was to be extended to gas workers nationally, railway workers and many others, whilst the older craft unions benefited greatly from the excitement and confidence engendered.

Annie Besant

Eleanor Marx

Tom Mann

Part 2
Explaining the upsurge

Social and economic conditions

UNSURPRISINGLY, LOW WAGES, long hours and awful working conditions were cited in the majority of cases where workers went on strike. Since these conditions were endemic they cannot really explain why and where strikes occurred when they did. When victimisation and a sense of injustice are added to the pot we have the fuel and the spark. This may be enough to account for the strikes which occurred in the decades following the collapse of Chartism. In this period industrial struggle was usually isolating and lonely. It was bitter and very hard fought in the face of a confident master class. It was often long lasting and enjoyed only modest success. It was also largely confined to skilled workers.

In the late 1880s events took a qualitatively different turn. As struggle followed struggle there was a sense of movement and continuity. The revolt of the unskilled dissolved sectional, ethnic and gender boundaries. It rose, peaked and collapsed in months, but it left an important legacy: the perception that those previously considered unorganisable could be organised and indeed could organise themselves. A purely economic explanation will not do.

A number of conditions came together at the end of the decade. There were the basic facts of exploitation and oppression, both longer term and immediate shifts in the economy, and the birth and activity of the new socialist movement. And it also appears that there was a special ingredient; the impact of Irish people and communities at a particular moment in the history of the isle's relationship with Britain.

The long term roots of the revolt lay in the appalling conditions meted out to working people in the obsessive drive to world power of the Victorian capitalist class. The Fabian, Beatrice Potter (Beatrice Webb), put the contradiction superbly. Writing of the docks and dock work in 1887, she said:

> Extremes meet and contrasts are intense. There is magnificence in the variety and costliness of the multitudinous wares handled by the most decrepit and poverty stricken worker — a hidden irony in his fate, touching all things and enjoying none. All the necessaries and most of the luxuries of our elaborate civilisation pass familiarly through the dock labourer's hands, or under his feet. The fine lady who sips her tea from a dainty cup, and talks sentimentally of the masses, is unaware that she is tangibly connected with them, in that the leaves from which her tea is drawn have been recently trodden into their case by a gang of the great unwashed.[41]

The relationship of domination and subordination of the capitalist class over the working class was established at work. A survey of the national income at the start of the new century showed that one third of it was taken by an upper class of 1.4 million and one third by a middle class of 4.1 million, leaving 39 million workers to share one third in wages. For the overwhelming majority of workers in work, there was not enough to cover the basic necessities of life.

The relationship was also experienced in the unsafe and unhealthy environment of the workplace. The camera brought one example to public notice. There is a haunting picture taken outside the Bryant and May match factory in Bow at the time of the strike. The pale-faced, early teenage girls all have a distended jaw line. They had phossey jaw, a cancer caused by handling phosphorous without protection.

Many workers' autobiographies report on the arrogant and superior attitudes of employers and their minions, the managers and foremen. They had the power of instant dismissal and used it freely. Will Thorne, the gas worker, was only eight, when:

> I was discharged from the brick works one morning, after I had been up two consecutive nights looking after slow fires, when the head foreman caught me asleep at about four o'clock and a number of the fires almost burnt out.[42]

A dismissal would pitch men, women and children onto the insecurity of the labour market where unemployment was a constant threat to all in a world where there were no state benefits. Here is an example from a Salvation Army survey of 1890:

> I'm a tailor. Have slept here [The Embankment] four nights running. Can't get work. Been out of a job three weeks. If I can muster cash I'll sleep at a lodging house...

> It was very wet last night. I left these seats and went to Covent Garden Market and kept under cover. There were about 30 of us. The police moved us on, but we went back as soon as they had gone. I've had a pen'orth of bread and pen'orth of soup during these last two days — often goes without altogether. There are women sleep out here. They are decent people, mostly charwomen and such who can't get work.[43]

So subordination reached out beyond the workplace to most aspects of the worker's life. The bulk of workers in the 1880s were still living in jerrybuilt rented accommodation in overcrowded and insanitary conditions. Writing of Manchester slums in 1889, Robert Blatchford reported that in the typical house:

> The [wall] paper is black with grease and grime of years, the plaster is cracked and crumbling, the ceilings are rent and swollen and foul, the woodwork is paintless, the roofs are broken, the walls damp, the doors and windows warped and shrunken, the rotten bricks and lath and plaster are reeking with pollution...[44]

Every industrial area had tens of thousands of dwellings to which Blatchford's description could have been applied. Such conditions fostered disease and poor health generally. Tuberculosis, the biggest killer, was rife in all working class communities. Medical practice was still in a very primitive state and hardly available at all to workers, except in its most basic form at charity hospitals or to those unfortunate enough to have applied to the workhouse. The workhouse was almost the ultimate hell for there it was policy to diminish the applicants sense of humanity in order to deter applications.

For several decades this situation had contributed to the emergence of a politically passive working class. Workers were worn down by long hours, inadequate nutrition, poor health and employer confidence. On the other hand, some workers fought back. There were many strikes across industry for economic goals. Endemic disease, crime and sectarian disorder had created a definite fear of the workers among the middle and upper classes. One aspect of this fear was the enormous growth of urban policing, what a Batley worker called, 'a plague of blue locusts', or, as the London tailor above, had it, there 'to move us on'.

Whilst this represents a generalised picture of workers' experience in the period, it is important to register its unevenness. The working class was fragmented. Some skilled and often unionised workers had gradually begun to enjoy an existence better than that of the mass of unskilled. They received higher and usually more regular earnings. This had allowed them to live in superior accommodation in different areas of town and to eat and dress better. They might also work shorter hours and have a margin of time and money for developing leisure activity.

This appears to have been generally true of Lancashire cotton towns from the end of the Cotton Famine in the mid-1860s. The late 70s and the 80s were notable for the emergence of professional football as a spectator sport, for the growth of the music hall as a popular entertainment and even for the establishment of the seaside holiday in resorts such as Blackpool. Friendly Society accounts show an increase in savings among workers. This is not to argue that such workers were satisfied with their lot. Far from it. Most of the countless industrial battles of mid-Victorian Britain were fought by skilled workers. Lancashire cotton workers had distinguished themselves by taking the side of the slaves in the American Civil War to their own immediate cost.

It is also important to register that if Lancashire textile workers in the period were enjoying generally rising living standards there were costs. Female and child labour at low wages helped to produce a higher family wage. However, long hours at the factory, plus rearing children and running the home damaged women's health and 'better off' Lancashire towns registered higher rates of infant mortality than comparable industrial areas in this period. And it is also clear that the good years were punctuated by bad ones where any savings were eaten up in making ends meet.

Despite the establishment of state education in 1870, the working class was lucky to get even the rudiments. The poorer areas of towns could expect less expenditure on buildings, teachers and materials. The condition of working arrangements in a particular area or industry could give local authorities the right to bend the rules. In the cotton towns, for example, children attended school only half time, since industry demanded a regular supply of cheap child labour, and so did the family economy. And labourers' children everywhere were encouraged to make an early contribution to the family economy to prevent the family becoming a charge on the Poor Law.

Inequality was a permanent feature of British society. It had been preserved by a combination of patronising arrogance from the rulers enforced by a growing network of policemen, poor law officials and teachers. Since the demise of the Chartists there had been no mass opposition to the system which produced it. Such an opposition developed in the late 1880s. Why did the situation change?

Firstly there was the question of the economy. Between 1850 and 1870 the British economy was pre-eminent in the world. There were almost two decades of continuous growth. However, from the 1870s it entered into a long period of uncertainty commencing with the onset of Depression in 1873. With the end of the American Civil War and the unification of Germany, Britain faced steeply rising competition for markets for raw materials and finished goods. Agriculture was particularly hard hit with a big downturn in commodity prices. Ireland and the rural areas of Britain were very hard hit. But so was British industry. The ruling class tried a battery of solutions. It embarked on a new phase of imperial conquest, especially in Africa. And there was also enormous investment in non-colonial countries like Argentina and Turkey in an attempt to check competitors. In some branches of industry there was intense technical and managerial innovation. There was a shift in investment from land into equities. Much of this meant problems for the working class. There was massive rural depopulation as agricultural workers flocked to the cities in search of work. When this long term trend converged with dips in the trade cycle, the result was rising unemployment and attempts at wage cutting. But there were also short periods of recovery and falling unemployment. Workers in work would grow more confident. They would seek improvement: for wage rises and shorter working hours. There was just such an economic upturn in 1888-89. Success bred success, as such demands ran through the poorer sections of society. Socialists connected with the changing mood.

The socialists

DURING THE HIGH POINT OF VICTORIAN prosperity from the 50s to the 80s life for socialists was very tough. After Chartism class struggle did not disappear as some have contended. There were countless strikes in many regions and industries. They were fought with great determination and much bitterness. They were fought largely by craftsmen in pursuit of sectional interest. They were not fertile ground for socialists. Nevertheless, the socialist tradition in Britain was kept alive by small propaganda and discussion groups around Marx and Engels and a few survivors of the Chartist phase.

The Great Depression, colonial adventure and repression in Ireland brought about a quickening of radical critiques of society. By the early 80s some of the old socialists with left wing liberals and younger converts grouped together to form a new Democratic Federation. This organisation has been seen as transitional between radicalism and socialism. Certainly, the political work which initially excited its adherents was not socialist. This was *Progress and Poverty,* by the American radical land reformer Henry George.[45] It sold 100,000 copies in its first year, 1881. Its central argument was land reform, to be achieved by the levying by the state of a 'single tax'. It had tremendous resonance for poor Irish farm tenants facing eviction and Scottish crofters suffering a renewed bout of 'clearances' by landlords creating vast deer runs in the Highlands for their own pleasure.[46] It also connected with the popular radical sentiment for land reform in England, running back at least to William Cobbett and Thomas Spence in the early years of the 19th century.[47] And it hit the topically raw spot created by large scale unemployment on the land.

Gladstone's policy of coercion towards Ireland evoked an outraged response in the Federation. It participated in a massive anti-government demonstration in Hyde Park. A large section of radicals withdrew from the new body because of its antagonism to the Liberal government. This made the way clearer for the socialists. The organisation moved into agitation on unemployment involving street corner meetings and demonstrations. It developed a social programme to complement the political demands of radicalism.

In 1884 its name was changed to the Social Democratic Federation. It was joined by the Labour Emancipation League, thus acquiring a number of members and branches in the East End of London. The Scottish Land and Labour League also affiliated, as did small groups in the Midlands and Yorkshire. At the beginning of 1884 a number of leading figures travelled to Blackburn to agitate round a great Lancashire cotton strike. They spoke at a rally of 1,500 and recruited nearly 100 members. The skeleton was formed of the first socialist organisation on a national basis.

The SDF did not, however, have an unproblematic start in life. Its campaigning street style on issues like Ireland and unemployment had brought into its ranks a wide range of activists. There were many different perspectives on issues and strategy. A fundamental difference existed over parliament and elections. The Federation's right wing argued for full participation whilst the left contended:

> The social inequality, the existence of a privileged and a poor class, is caused not by an inadequate extension of the franchise...but by the class appropriation of the means and material of making wealth... Parliament is a mere sham of governing.[48]

But there was also the attitude of the SDF's leading figure, Henry Mayers Hyndman. He was a Tory gentleman who turned to socialism whilst maintaining some strongly reactionary attitudes. He claimed to be the first British advocate of Marxism, though he infuriated Marx and Engels by failing to acknowledge his debt to Marx in his book *England for All.* However, he saw British socialism as national in character. He strongly favoured the survival and expansion of the empire. He was for Home Rule for Ireland but within the empire, was anti-Semitic and was distinctly elitist in his attitude to working class members. Yet he claimed to favour social revolution!

Furthermore, he exercised personal control over the organisation through the paper, *Justice.* Matters came to a head rapidly and after the 1884 annual conference a left faction broke away to form the Socialist League. This included a number of the outstanding socialist figures of the time, amongst whom were William Morris, Karl Marx's youngest daughter, Eleanor, her partner Edward Aveling, and John Lincoln Mahon, a young skilled engineer. There was also a group of anarchists. The split took place with the strong support of Frederick Engels who had no faith in Hyndman's ability to build a revolutionary organisation

The organisations found themselves in competition with each other especially in agitational work on unemployment, free speech and Ireland and they also met each other when campaigning among workers struggling for unionisation. In these early days of the socialist movement there was still a good deal of fluidity between groups before future battle lines had been firmly drawn. Some of the leading figures freely co-operated with each other despite their different affiliations. George Bernard Shaw, the playwright, who had joined the Fabian Society[49] at its inception, also in 1884, attended meetings of the Socialist League throughout its life, and participated in several campaigns apparently without sectarian intent.

It is important to register that both the SDF and SL were small organisations and were to remain so throughout the 80s. Their total membership probably never exceeded 1,000 at any one time, though many more passed through the organisations. Indeed the SL only just survived the decade after furious factional rows and defections. Ultimately it was hijacked by anarchists.

The bulk of the membership of both groups was London based, though their leading activists travelled widely, making contact with socialists and workers in many places. Recruitment could be substantial but consolidation was usually beyond them. They had neither the political experience, the theoretical coherence nor the methodology to maintain their organisational integrity in a turbulent decade.

Sharp political differences marked their early lives as organisations. The milieu from which they came guaranteed they would be preyed upon by a range of fads such as spiritualism, occultism and phrenology. Even without such exotic diversions, as the first British socialist organisations, they would be the first to deal with some of the big real questions for socialists. These included: how to navigate the parliamentary road, reform or revolution, how to relate to existing political parties and the ramifications of the trade union question. There was a lot of internal mudslinging. Yet despite the handicaps they had an impact upon events far beyond what their size would suggest.

Their strong point was outdoor activity: paper sales, street meetings, processions and demonstrations. It is striking to note just how frequent these activities were. From the start in 1884 street meetings were a regular part of activity, taking place virtually every Sunday. Wholesale newsagents had blocked the sale of *Justice* through normal channels, so the SDF members set out to sell on the streets. Jack Williams, a working class activist, wrote:

> There was Hyndman, in his immaculate frock coat and high hat; there was Morris, dressed in his usual blue serge suit and soft hat; Champion looking every inch the military man; Joynes in his aesthetic dress; Frost looking every

inch the aristocrat; Quelch and myself in our everyday working clothes. I am sure we made an impression...[50]

In London, where most of this activity was concentrated, both the SDF and the League had pitches in central and east London and the League two in Hammersmith. Their presence irritated the authorities who worried about the growth of socialist ideas and the involvement of working men and women. A determined effort was made to stop such activity.

In May 1885 the police attacked the International Club in central London, breaking windows, destroying and stealing property and arresting members. As the movement responded it was greeted by a round of harassment, arrests, fines and jailings, the majority of which were working class members. The SL and the SDF joined with some radical groups to build a large demonstration in protest.

In September 1885 thousands were drawn to Dod Street in Limehouse in the heart of dockland. After a very successful rally with many defiant speeches the meeting was closed. A large force of police laid into the dispersing crowd, arresting eight people and injuring many more. At the subsequent court hearing those arrested were jailed or fined. The next week up to 50,000 people turned up. This was repeated the following week. After this the campaign switched its attention to Bell Street, Edgware Road, in the summer of 1886. Leading members of the groups were arrested and jailed but by the end of that summer the police had backed off. The campaign had had at least temporary success just by sheer force of numbers. Of course it says a good deal for both organisations that they could repeatedly pull such large and sympathetic crowds to defend the right of socialists to put their point of view on the street.

If the Free Speech Campaign brought relations with the police to a head, it was the campaigns on unemployment and in sympathy with the Irish which had provoked the violent harassment in the first place. In February 1886 a large crowd met in Trafalgar Square to hear militant speeches from SDF speakers. Following the speeches, John Burns, carrying a red flag, led the crowd from Hyde Park up Pall Mall into gentlemen's clubland. Jeered by gents and stoned by their servants, the crowd took out their class hatred on the club premises by window smashing followed by looting the luxury shops on Oxford Street.

The press and politicians entered into an orgy of condemnation. As E P Thompson wrote, 'All the submerged class fears and hatred of the bourgeoisie suffered nearly a week of naked exposure.'[51] The national charity for the unemployed grew massively in the wake of the riot (£75,000 in 48 hours!). Unemployment demonstrations and rioting took place in Leicester, where they lasted for five days. William Morris stood bail for the SDF members arrested and wrote:

> What was the meaning of it? At bottom misery, illuminated by a faint glimmer of hope, raised by the magic word SOCIALISM, the only hope of these days of confusion. That was what the crowd represented, whatever other elements were mingled with it.[52]

The new socialists were at their best on the streets. Courageous and provocative from the platform, they made connections with the poor and downtrodden population of London and several provincial communities. On Easter Sunday 1887 the socialists participated in what Engels called 'without exception the largest meeting we've ever had here'. The gathering was to protest against the renewal of the Crimes Bill which would virtually remove all civil rights from the Irish — 150,000 people gathered in Hyde Park to hear speakers from 15 platforms. They came from all over London in vast converging contingents. Some suffered police harassment, but the sheer numbers involved seem to have acted as a restraint upon police assaults.

In the late summer, however, the authorities once more stepped up their attacks. A new Tory government was determined to establish its authority on the streets, particularly in the light of a fresh phase of nationalist activity in Ireland and the sympathy the Irish were inspiring in Britain. The callous right wing press commended the signs of firmness across the Atlantic where six framed anarchists were about to be executed in Chicago. This followed the the previous year's Chicago May Day demonstration in Haymarket Square, when a bomb had been thrown by an *agent provocateur* after the rally had ended. The indicted men had not even been present when the bomb exploded. There was also praise in the press for Bismarck who had brought in Anti-Socialist Laws in Germany to try to crush the growing influence of the Social Democrats.

The new Commissioner of the Metropolitan Police, the former colonial governor, Sir Charles Warren, banned all meetings in Trafalgar Square. His officers carried out weeks of harassment and summary arrest throughout the capital.

The Radicals and the Irish called a demonstration in Trafalgar Square for 13 November, the day after the execution of the Haymarket Martyrs in Chicago and the day before the Crimes Bill was to get the Royal Assent. Socialists threw themselves into this activity with gusto, forming contingents in various parts of the East End. Thousands of police armed with long truncheons, cutlasses and firearms were massed in the Square. There were also squads in the streets round it. The demonstrators came from several directions. They were attacked savagely before they reached the Square but in panicky retreat could only enter it, where they were set upon and thrashed. One observer, Liberal MP Sir E Reed, wrote of the arrest of the radical-socialist MP for Lanark, Cunningham-Grahame:

> After Mr Grahame's arrest was complete one policeman after another, two certainly, but I think no more, stepped up from behind and struck him on the head from behind with a violence and brutality which were shocking to behold. Even after this, and when some some five or six other police were dragging him into the Square, another from behind seized him most needlessly by the hair...and dragged his head back, and in that condition he was forced many yards.[53]

This episode, known immediately as 'Bloody Sunday', did not, as the hysterical press expected, intimidate the movement. It seemed inspired to retaliate. Demonstrators were out in force the next Sunday and subjected to further wild police attacks. During such an attack a young radical clerk, Alfred Linnell, was run down by a police horse, dying later in hospital. His funeral became a major political event organised by the socialists. It was attended by most of the leading figures on the left, but more importantly by tens of thousands of east Londoners on a procession which was lined by many thousands more. William Morris spoke at the graveside:

> Our friend who lies here has had a hard life and met with a hard death; and if society had been differently constituted, his life might have been a delightful, a beautiful and a happy one. It is our business to begin to organise for the purpose of seeing that such things shall not happen; to try and make this earth a beautiful and happy place.[54]

Street activity was meat and drink to this first generation of socialists. And they were good at it. Success was partly due, no doubt, to their very newness and enthusiasm in an increasingly promising climate. Their political centres were weak but this could actually be an asset where immensely talented individuals could make brilliant interventions without interference. Two examples might be cited.

In 1887 John Lincoln Mahon, notionally of the Socialist League, undertook an organising and propaganda campaign for socialism among the striking miners of Northumberland. Mahon was a young engineering worker who had joined the Federation at its inception. Blacklisted by employers, he had thrown himself with massive enthusiasm into rolling agitation. He had gone with the SL in the split but continued to work with SDF members in action. In the months before meeting the Northumberland miners he had visited chain-makers on strike in Cradley Heath and Walsall, and spoken at meetings in Leicester, Nottingham,

Oxford, Norwich and Lancashire. He was convinced that 'branches might be formed in nearly every town in England if only some energetic organisers could be sent round to give things a start.'[55]

He arrived in Northumberland where the miners had been on strike trying to resist a 12½ percent wage cut. The miners came in hundreds and even thousands to hear the socialist message. Both Morris and Hyndman addressed thousands in a field near Blyth after marching six miles: 'through the dreary (O so dreary) villages, & that terrible waste of endless backyard, we could see on our left hand a strip of the bright blue sea, forming a strange border to the misery of the land'.[56]

Another young engineer, Tom Mann, went to Northumberland to work for the SDF. He had started 18 branches in the Northumberland coalfield by the start of 1888, the largest of them in Ashington with 100 members claimed. Only the Newcastle one survived into the 90s. Mann's work was undertaken despite a major dispute with Hyndman over trade union work.

As we have seen, Mann was a key figure in the Great Dock Strike in the summer of 1889. He acted as treasurer and picket organiser, both very successful operations. And John Burns, also a member of the SDF, was the most publicly prominent of the strike leaders, though also an engineer. By this time the SL was a warring husk of an organisation, but the SDF was growing. Its best year was 1887, the year of the Northumberland miners' struggle and the great London demonstrations. It peaked at 783 members in 39 branches.

It fell back a little in 1888, but won more than 100 members in 40 branches in 1889. However, it fell back again in 1890 by perhaps a quarter to 453 members in 34 branches.[57] SDF members were active in the strike, in fact they were indispensable to its success, but the 'party' gave no guidance to its members whatever. Hyndman was even negative about it. Mann and Burns were active despite their 'party' membership.

Another reason for their success was the absence of competition. The Northumberland miners were organised. The coalfield was the base for miner Thomas Burt's 13 year old hold on the Morpeth parliamentary seat in the Liberal interest. It was the cradle of Lib-Labism, the alliance of trade union leaders and the Liberal Party which gave the former a few seats in parliament. Burt's success had come on the back of a fiercely combative franchise campaign by the miners after the 1867 Reform Act. During the 1887 conflict Burt, probably because of his Liberal affiliations, was hostile to the strikers' militancy and the strikers were hostile to him. This made it easier for the socialists to get a hearing. So the circumstances were special.

Normally it was where trade unionism was weak or nonexistent that the socialists could make the strongest intervention. Such situations were a test of their energy, enthusiasm and ability to identify immediately with the workers' needs. The most celebrated struggles for New Unionism — the Match Girls, the gas workers and the dockers — were ideal sites for the use of these qualities. People like Mahon, Burns, Mann and Will Thorne, the gas worker, possessed them in abundance. And the circumstances were ideal for the involvement of the middle class members such as Eleanor Marx and Edward Aveling. There was no exhausting contest with the entrenched trade union old guard and its relationship with Liberalism.

So many of the new socialists engaged with the industrial struggles of the late 80s with enthusiasm and effect. They fed, accommodated and deployed pickets, organised processions, ran offices, collected money, spoke on street corners and took the strikers' story to the public through their papers and leaflets. In the cases of gas workers and dockers success would not have come without the socialists. Yet, for all that, they did not build a large and successful socialist organisation based on the principles of class struggle.

Effective though the work was round strikes, it also had limitations. It was largely an extension of their other major activity, open air meetings and demonstrations round specific issues. Such an appearance would be consistent with 'theoretical' positions taken by the organisations since their inception. Both organisations had a proper disrespect for the leaders of the craft unions but both subsumed the entire membership of those unions under that leadership's goals. They failed to comment on the fact that Mann, Burns and Mahon, all leading members and socialist activists, were also engineers and members of the ASE. This lack of interest in trade unionism as represented by the craft unions tended to be extended to include trade unionism in general.

Strikes were recognised as legitimate workers' activity, and ones which should usually be encouraged. They were handy forums for the making of revolutionary socialist propaganda, not central elements in the class struggle. During strikes the papers (*Justice* and *Commonweal*) took little interest in the issues or dynamics of the conflict or of their impact upon ruling class interests. They tended to lecture the workers on the need for socialist revolution. Engels was especially critical of this revolutionary posturing. We must exclude activists like Tom Mann from some of these strictures. He was certainly deeply interested in the dynamics and success of strikes. For him clearly the nuts and bolts of the action were critical.

At the time of the dock strike Mann was still a member of the SDF though alienated from the leadership and from Hyndman in particular. For three years he had been directing his energies to building a movement round the demand for the eight hour day. It had started with the writing of his first pamphlet, *What a Compulsory Eight Hour Day Means to the Workers.* He saw the issue as a critical one for uniting workers. The pamphlet ended with a call to:

> Liberal and Tory, christian and free thinker, unionist and non-unionist, mechanic and labourer, radical and social-democrat, teetotaller or vegetarian, whatsoever your creed or sex, [to] unite on common ground and let us fight this battle of the workers with vigour, with energy and determination... The result will be a hastening of that glorious time when the domination of a class shall be a matter of history and when all shall have enough work and none shall have too much.[58]

Tom Mann was grasping the centrality of finding issues, from within working class experience, which could unite the maximum number of workers. This was placing him ahead of many of his colleagues in the SDF/SL. Mann's campaign had some success on the ground, especially in south London. Eventually it was to be embraced by the TUC.

He had a warm and affectionate relationship with William Morris and Eleanor Marx, but by 1889 the League was in the hands of anarchists and was sectarian. Eleanor was completely oriented upon industrial struggles and Morris, whatever his theoretical scepticism was always drawn by a strike's excitement and vigour. He wrote of what he called 'the labourers revolt in the East End':

> ...this is a revolt against oppression: a protest against the brute force which keeps a huge population down in the depths of the most dire degradation, for the benefit of a knot of profit-hunters...this is a strike of the poor against the rich.

Morris seemed to have grasped the essential character of that upsurge in a manner matched only by Engels. Of the general strike call he said, 'The mere fact that it was thought possible to bring about a general strike in London remains the central point in the history of the strike.'[59]

William Morris was a sensitive and acute observer and a brilliant propagandist for socialist ideas. His novel News from Nowhere is a wonderful romp into the future. It contains debates upon many vital issues for socialists written in a light and accessible manner: parliament, revolution, art, human relations. Morris had no doubts about the need for revolutionary change through class struggle. He wrote:

> ...the contrasts of rich and poor are unendurable and ought not to be endured... Now it seems to me that, feeling this, I am bound to act for the destruction of the

system which seems to me mere oppression and obstruction; such a system can only be destroyed, it seems to me, by the united discontent of numbers; isolated acts of a few persons of the upper and middle classes seeming to me quite powerless against it; in other words, the antagonism of classes, which the system had bred, is the natural and necessary instrument of its destruction.[60]

From the moment Morris 'found' socialism, as the answer to the society of ugliness and twisted values, he became its tireless advocate. Between 1883 and 1890 he was the most active propagandist in Britain, addressing over 1,000 meetings, and his articles were read by thousands. 'Every group of socialists included some who had been converted by his words',[61] and he did not occupy the armchair. He travelled to the Northumberland miners' strike in 1887, speaking to a mass meeting and engaging with the miners. He was present at most of the big East End demonstrations during the decade, was ready to fight and turned up provocatively at the police courts in support of those arrested.

Morris remains one of the most attractive figures in the history of socialism in Britain. However, it must be recorded that he failed to use his immense talents to build an effective organisation. He showed no capacity to fight for an organisation even when he saw wrong directions being taken. Despite his great prestige and following in the early socialist movement, he gave no lead. At the moment of the upsurge of militancy at the end of the 1880s this became a serious matter.

John Burns, also in the dock strike leadership, though

nominally still a member of the SDF, was working with H H Champion in the Labour Electoral Association. There was a developing tendency in the movement to follow the parliamentary road. So, effectively, there was no revolutionary socialist 'party' to draw strikers into. This meant that much of the energy and activity built up by thousands of workers in the strike movement would be dissipated when the strikes were over.

So we are left with a real paradox. Socialists led the great strike movement of the late 80s which produced the New Unions. It was their work over the previous years in the East End of London, and on a smaller scale elsewhere, which gave them a relationship with newly militant workers. Many of these workers would have taken part in the processions and demonstrations, again led by socialists, which had become a regular feature of central and east and south London life in the 80s. As Engels wrote in 1890:

> The movement which I now consider irrepressible, arose from the dock strike, purely out of the absolute necessity of defence. But here too the ground had been so far prepared by the various forms of agitation in the last eight years that the people without being socialists themselves, still wanted to have only socialists as their leaders.[62]

Yet the main socialist organisations were tiny, swinging between reformism and ultra-leftism. They were led by Hyndman, a vainglorious bigot, and William Morris, whose instincts were excellent, but who, whilst always a party member, had no real commitment to party building. Their papers carried propaganda, sometimes of high quality, but failed to connect with actual workers' struggles and concerns. What is really remarkable, considering the handicaps, is that a few dedicated socialists achieved so much.

The Irish

Ireland and the Irish run like a tough green thread through the politics and society of Britain. In 1870 Marx had written:

> Ireland is the bulwark of the English landed aristocracy. The exploitation of this country is not only one of the main sources of that aristocracy's material welfare; it is its greatest moral strength. It, in fact, represents the domination of England over Ireland. Ireland is therefore the great means by which the English aristocracy maintains its domination in England itself...
>
> As for the English bourgeoisie it has in the first place a common interest with the English aristocracy in turning Ireland into mere pasture land which provides the English market with meat and wool at the cheapest possible prices. It is equally interested in reducing by eviction and forcible emigration, the Irish population to such a small number that English capital can function there with security...
>
> ...owing to the constantly increasing concentration of

> farming, Ireland steadily supplies its own surplus to the English labour market, and thus forces down wages and lowers the moral and material condition of the English working class...
>
> And most important of all! Every industrial and commercial centre in England now possesses a working class divided into two hostile camps, English proletarians and Irish proletarians. The ordinary English worker hates the Irish worker as a competitor who lowers his standard of life. In relation to the Irish worker he feels himself a member of the ruling nation and turns himself into a tool of the aristocrats and capitalists of his country thus strengthening their domination over himself.

Marx was writing in the aftermath of the Fenian rising in the 60s.[63] A decade on, it was no less true. But by the end of the 1880s the situation had begun to open up. Nationalist tactics in Ireland, the emerging of an English socialist movement and the upsurge of the unskilled workers, vast numbers of whom were Irish, promised to produce a fresh slant on the Irish question.

Ireland was firmly back on the agenda of British politics in the 1880s. Irish peasants suffered severely in the Great Depression. Their profits hit by falling world prices for agricultural goods, landlords tried to make up their deficits by increasing rents and enacting evictions. The Irish resisted. Successive governments meted out savage punishments. Irish rebels brought the struggle to the mainland in a spate of bombings. This was met by repression and victimisation, largely in Ireland.

It is reasonable to suppose that the droves of Irish men

and women compelled to leave their homes left with at least a deep sense of grievance aimed at landlords, agents, magistrates and other petty officials, policemen, soldiers, politicians and government — all faces of 'The Protestant Ascendancy'. We know that from the masses of migrants who went to America, at any time from the 1840s, came tens of thousands of generous donations to support the most recent victims of oppression in Ireland and the people and bodies which organised resistance. In this period the Land League was a major recipient of support, as, a little later, was the Irish National League. Although harder to document, so were the underground organisations — the surviving Fenians, the Irish Republican Brotherhood and the Ribbon Societies. Although masses of American Irish remained poor with limited resources, in a burgeoning economy less 'caste ridden' than Britain many did find work and prospered. Furthermore with the Atlantic between them and Dublin Castle there was little to fear from recrimination. They openly proclaimed and celebrated their Irishness, their nationalism and their republicanism.

For the Irish in Glasgow, Liverpool, Manchester, Leeds, Tyneside and London the experience was very different. They were at the bottom. They were crowded into unspeakable housing — often cold, lightless, waterlogged basements or cellars — in the most insanitary districts in the urban landscape. They scrambled for casual, unskilled work: loading and unloading, lifting and carrying, shovelling, digging, tunnelling and stoking. Last to be taken on. First to be laid off. Treated with contempt. Subject to violent prejudice and discrimination. Watched and harassed by the police and the Poor Law Guardians. Condemned for violence and ignorance and blamed for crime and the carrying of disease. They were unorganised and apparently unorganisable.

Yet it was from the workplaces inhabited by the Irish that much of the great trade union upsurge of the late 1880s came. Over half of Britain's dockers were Irish or of Irish extraction. Similarly, others worked in the filthy, malodorous world of the gas industry. Both areas formed the spearhead of New Unionism. But of course it was not a *new* world. Something significant was happening in the consciousness of these poor workers at that time. There was a recession. The impact of poverty was certainly intensified. But how far was there an 'Irish' dimension?

The high profile of Ireland and the policy zig-zags of successive governments gave the emerging radical and socialist organisations of the decade an issue around which to organise. Since 'the land question' was a major preoccupation of these circles in the 70s and 80s, the land question's Irish dimension fitted radical and socialist propaganda very well. In the periods when he was not under arrest or in detention, Michael Davitt campaigned among British trade unionists and socialists. Davitt was a veteran of the Fenian struggles of the 60s. At a mass rally in Hyde Park in June 1885, he said:

> The industrial classes in these countries can, if they combine at the polls, hurl the party of wars and waste, of land monopoly and the plunder of labour...from the helm of state, and substitute government of the people and by the people... Demand universal adult suffrage...the nationalisation of agriculture and pasture

land...the municipalisation of land on which centres of population stand...state ownership of the mines...eight hours per day...abolition of the hereditary chamber of obstruction, the House of Lords, and finally demand that atonement be made to Ireland for the crimes which your statesmen have been guilty of...by restoring to her the right to manage her own affairs in a national assembly in Dublin.[64]

Davitt was tireless in his attempts to overcome prejudice by campaigning on issues central to the needs of English workers linking them to the problem of Ireland. He was an enthusiast for labour representation. He assisted Keir Hardie in his first election campaign in Mid-Lanark in 1887. And the English radicals and socialists reciprocated. In 1887, led by the young George Lansbury, a delegation of 12 visited Ireland 'to see what crimes were being committed in their name'. So there were ongoing relations between Irish radicals and the emerging British workers' movement.

In April 1887 a reported 150,000 people demonstrated in Hyde Park against Balfour's Crimes Bill. Although Gladstone was a principal speaker and Michael Davitt represented the Nationalists, most of the other speakers were socialists, including George Bernard Shaw and Eleanor Marx, wearing green. Then, in November of '87, a further mass rally took place in Trafalgar Square despite a Metropolitan Police Commissioner's ban, to protest at arrests in Ireland under the new act. The arrests had followed the murder by police of three demonstrators in Mitchelstown, County Cork. The London police went berserk, injuring 200 demonstrators in an attempt to clear the Square. The event became known in the movement as 'Bloody Sunday'.

The socialists had been campaigning on the Irish issue for months. In January 1887 thousands had turned up on Clerkenwell Green to protest at the spate of fresh evictions in Ireland. From the reports of the April demonstration we know that great contingents marched from Poplar, Rotherhithe, Bermondsey and Deptford – all dockland areas and all areas with high concentrations of the Irish. It seems highly probable that large contingents from such areas to a demonstration on an Irish issue would consist largely of the Irish.[65]

In mid-80s London demonstrations and mass meetings had become a regular part of the capital's life. In 1885 the socialists organised a Free Speech Movement against harassment of speakers by the Metropolitan Police. In September some 60,000 turned out in the Dod Street area where Eleanor Marx, John Burns and William Morris had been speaking regularly for months. Dod Street is in Poplar, close to the West India Docks where the Great Strike was to begin in August 1889. Throughout 1886, '87, '88 and '89 demonstrations were held regularly on a range of issues including unemployment, fees paid by scholars and the demand for an eight hour day. The socialists of the Socialist League and the SDF were the organisers of many of such events and, from the mid-80s had branches in the East End dockland areas.

Regular meetings, demonstrations, street sales, ale house and street corner arguments were a welcome part of working class life. Comfortable homes, TV, cinema and football, as staples of life in our own time, can make us forget just how much of life in the past was spent out of doors: on the street, in the park, on the common. Apart from the bitter cold and wet of the winter months the home, overcrowded, dark, cold and often damp, was much less attractive than outdoors. Processions, demonstrations and open air meetings were a welcome diversion from the grimness and tedium of much of domestic and working life. It is quite likely that the dockers and their families who took part in the daily trek through the city behind John Burns's straw hat, in the first two weeks of the strike in 1889, were actually used to such activity.

Through regular social contact in the communities, opinions on the great issues of the day would pass into common currency. For the Irish, such opinions would be tempered and shaped by a particular range of experiences. George Lansbury, a future Labour Party leader, was brought up in the East End. He was a child at the time of the Fenian activities in the 1860s. In his autobiography he wrote:

> The Irish boys at our school were all 'Fenians'; consequently, when the wall of Clerkenwell Prison was blown down and three Irish martyrs executed in Manchester because a police officer was accidentally killed, very great excitement prevailed in our classes and playground. The teachers tried to make us believe how wicked the Irishmen had been on both occasions, but my Irish friends would have none of it, and when a few months later T D Sullivan's song *God Save Ireland* came out, we boys were shouting it at the tops of our voices every playtime.[66]

The 'spontaneous' movement of the 'apathetic' dockland masses in August 1889 is never really explained, except in terms of the exactions of life in the docks. But exactions had always been there. It was true that 1889 was one of those rare points where the demand for labour in the docks actually outstripped supply. This must have increased confidence. But, additionally, what seems to have been happening in the 80s was a growing participation in a vibrant political culture through involvement in street corner meetings and mass demonstrations. Weaned on hatred for the British state — or rather its various agents — the Irish would be excellent material for initiating and participating in this upsurge. A figure of over 60 percent has been given for Irishmen in the dock labour force. The advent of New Unionism at the end of the 80s gave structure and purpose to feelings. Llewellyn Smith said, 'Until the recent dock strike the only really well-organised body of labourers in East London was the Stevedores' Union, manned and officered by London Irish; and a very large proportion of the strike committee during the dock strike were of Irish extraction.'[67] The list of names given by Tillett, in his autobiography, suggests that at least a third were Irish. And the appointed meeting place, the Wade Arms, was an Irish owned pub.

The Irish connection was even stronger in Liverpool, the first port of call for many Irish migrants and the place of settlement for large numbers since the 1840s. There the dock labour force was even more Irish than London. Two members of the Irish Land League, Edward McHugh and Richard McGhee, friends of Michael Davitt, had founded a union on the Glasgow docks in 1889. This was the National Union of Dock Labourers. Probably influenced by the success of the London strike, but affected by similar grievances, Liverpool dockers struck for a month at the beginning of 1890. McHugh and McGhee brought their union to Liverpool, recruiting widely. The union failed to win recognition in a strike which Davitt played a part in settling. Nevertheless it hung on to produce viable organisation with 6,000 members by 1891, half of whom were recruited during the strike.

It has been estimated that only one in ten Catholics attended mass in London in the 80s and there appears to be a rather similar figure for Liverpool.[68] P J Waller says, 'A majority of Catholics was indifferent about expressing their faith by attendance at church.' However, the figures do not tell all. The Liverpool strike was visited by Tom Mann and Cunningham-Grahame. The dockers were warned by the Catholic hierarchy of the alien ideas expressed by such men. There is no evidence of much success for the socialist outsiders and Liverpool was to remain a difficult pitch for socialists for a considerable time. This was probably as much a result of sectarianism engendered by Orange organisations as the influence of the Church.

In the London strike Cardinal Manning played a key role. He is mentioned in an East End context in strike leaders' accounts even before the strike's beginning. Presumably, that he could play a role at all derived from his confidence that dock workers were substantially Roman Catholic, if not regularly taking Mass. His potential impact on rank and file dockers and their families was possibly understood very well by convinced secularists like Burns and Mann and the sceptical Tillett. Yet none of them publicly evinced anything but gratitude for the role His Eminence had played. His self consciously moderating influence was to go unchallenged.

Manning's defenders outside and often inside the labour movement have always presented his role as entirely benign and disinterested. But his agenda was broader than merely 'standing on the side of labour' as one biographer characterised it. He had long been an organiser within the Catholic community. In 1872 he had founded the League of the Cross, a temperance organisation modelled on the tactics of the Salvation Army. Within two years it claimed 28,000 members and in 1890 there were 42 branches led by 80 priests in the dioceses of Westminster and Southwark. He said, in 1890, 'The League [has] taken hold of the people, especially the working men. It was this that gave me a hold in the Dock Strike of last year.'[69]

The power of the Catholic hierarchy, stated or understated, was a very significant factor in understanding the impact of the Irish in British politics in the 19th century and possibly well into the 20th. Apart from the celebrated Manning intervention, in 1879 the Roman Catholic Bishop of Liverpool had issued a letter to be read in all parishes condemning strikers when the first Liverpool waterfront strike took place.

However, hierarchy or no hierarchy, Irishmen and women could bring to politics and trade unionism their hatred of British authority, 'scored with acid'.[70] In the development of mass politics in the 80s it was a very potent force and one which was of central importance to the flowering of New Unionism. The spirit of the Irish in the 80s may well have been the key factor in launching the mass movement. Paradoxically, however, it may well have been its Irishness, its relationship to Catholic authority which proved its downfall.

To carry that spirit and antagonism forward in fighting for socialism was a task of a different order. A central core of ideology had to be confronted head on. This required the building of a mass socialist organisation. On the other hand, once rudimentary organisation was established, that antagonism could be very serviceable for Labourism with its developing genius for compromise with the enemy. Ultimately, many of the areas of original New Union strength fell to the Independent Labour Party.

PART 3
The mass movement

Dockers' demonstration in the East End

Runaway consciousness

For a period, from spring 1889 to spring 1891 and peaking in August, the working class demonstrated a sort of 'runaway consciousness'. Although there were precedents, the Beckton mass recruitment and the Great Dock Strike have been claimed as the midwife of New Unionism. But it is not necessary to separate them nor is it really possible. They overlapped in time—March to September 1889. They overlapped in place—the strike began at the West India Dock just a mile or so from Beckton. As we have seen from the Match Girls' dispute a year earlier it is likely that family members took part in both. Certainly neighbours must have done. Their leaders interlocked—Thorne, Burns, Tillett, Champion, Mann. Eleanor Marx and Annie Besant were involved with many disputes. Most had worked together as socialist agitators for years. Many had had their heads bashed by policemen's truncheons. Their papers reported the progress of the movement and circulated in the community.

The decision to call a general strike in London made on

28 August and revoked a day later, was scorned by contemporaries. Historians have almost universally echoed that view, notwithstanding the fact that the main source of that opinion was the account of Llewellyn Smith and Vaughan Nash who were middle class 'friends of labour'. They suggest that the context was desperation:

> Hunger had played havoc in the ranks of the men; women and children were thinner and paler than a week ago. One by one the bits of furniture were disappearing at the pawnbrokers', and the grief and despair in many of the dockers' homes contrasted grimly with the gay banners and lively tunes of the daily processions through the city. The processions *kept up the numbers,* but an *experienced eye* could detect that there were *fewer and fewer dockers in their ranks* [my italics – JC]...the fortunes of the strikers touched low-water mark that evening. The 'no work manifesto' [general strike – JC] was, in truth a counsel of despair.[71]

Probing a little further we find that, according to Tillett, in his absence the decision to draft the strike manifesto was reached by as many as 50 men attending the strike committee.[72] The implication of Llewellyn Smith's account (the standard one on which most subsequent ones are based) was that it was the work of Burns, Mann and H H Champion. They probably were the authors, but there had clearly been a long discussion involving a lot of activists. Tillett reports that he was awoken in the small hours by Mann asking for his signature, which he appended, 'heavy with sleep and exhaustion'. Writing 40 years later, he says when he woke he realised, '[it] had to be withdrawn. It tended to alienate public sympathy.'

(NB curiously these are the exact words of *The Times* on Saturday 31 August 1889!).[73]

Tillett says, 'We had long and harassing discussions' ...with the strike committee leading to overturning the decision. Did someone else get to Tillett (and maybe Mann) early that morning undermining his/their own ambivalence? Someone with authority? Possibly someone 'haunted' by 'the fear that some fool or madman might step in'? One of Manning's biographers says that Margaret Harkness, the writer/journalist, formerly in the SDF and active in the strike, had been in touch with Cardinal Manning throughout the strike. Manning had visited the Lord Mayor to discuss the strike on 29 August.[74]

Is it not possible that Tom Mann and the rest of the strike committee arrived at the decision to make the call because of what they knew about the area over the past two weeks? There is some interesting evidence here. Running parallel with the dock strike and lasting till the end of September 1889 was a strike of Jewish tailoring workers. Its centre was Stepney, the district adjacent, and to the west, of Canning Town. It was a big and militant strike of over 6,000 workers with 120 workshops reported idle. Like so many of the strikes in the period it was led by members of the SDF who had been agitating among the tailors since 1885. The tailors had been very active in the movement against unemployment.

At a mass meeting on 26 August a manifesto was drawn up pledging to join in 'the general demand for increased comfort and shorter hours of labour', and demanding a reduction of hours, meal breaks, trade union rates from government contractors and a ban on government contractors and sweaters handing out home work. It finished with an appeal for all tailors' and tailoresses' 'support in joining this General Strike'. Posters in Yiddish and English appeared on street walls. Daily marches took place to Victoria Park to hear guest speakers including Tom Mann, John Burns and Ben Tillett. The dockers' strike committee answered the tailors' appeal for help with £100. The strike was settled in the workers' favour at the end of September.[75]

As significant as the tailors' strike, but never referred to in detail, was an amazing proliferation of disputes in the second half of August and the beginning of September. Within a rough triangle between the City, King's Cross and Blackwall, points roughly five miles apart, there were over 50 strikes in industries other than the docks. Outside that triangle in south and west London there were at least a further 16.[76] There was also a report of a rent strike on Commercial Road. 'As we are on strike landlords need not call' warned a banner over Hungerford Street with the accompanying rhyme:

Our husbands are on strike; for the wives it is not honey
And we all think it is not right to pay the landlord money.
Everyone is on strike; so landlords do not be offended.
The rent that's due we'll pay when the strike is ended.[77]

It is surely obvious that London was in ferment. Contemporaries knew it. On 27 August *The Evening News and Post* said, 'The proverbial small spark has kindled a great fire which threatens to envelop the whole metropolis.' On the 31st *The East London Advertiser* warned that 'strike operations [had] such general proportions as to make the rising a war between capitals and labour', whilst on 7 September *The East London News*'s main editorial was headed STRIKE FEVER and argued that 'the present week might not inaptly be called the week of strikes—coal men, Match Girls, parcels postmen, carmen, rag, bone and paper porters and pickers and the employees in jam, biscuit, rope, iron, screw, clothing and railway works have found some grievance, real and imaginary and have followed the infectious example of coming out on strike.' Further afield the *Newcastle Daily Courant*, on 27 August, told its readers that 'all kinds of workmen, far removed from the docks are joining the movement.' And from Bristol, on the 28th, *The Western Daily Press* stated that 'the great strike of dock labourers has reached enormous dimensions. The infection has spread to other classes of labouring men and the result is that London is threatened with a state of siege as if a hostile fleet held the entrance to the Thames'.

And, of course, the labour leaders knew it too. The dockers' strike committee had issued a statement only two days before the strike manifesto which read, 'We, the undersigned, strongly deprecate the rash action taken by unorganised workmen not directly connected with the dock work of coming out on strike without reflecting that by doing so they are increasing the strain upon the strike committee's resources. Organisation must precede strikes, or failure is certain.'

Three matters are raised. The first is how the committee could come to such a dramatically different decision 48 hours later. It is difficult to know with any certainty but it does seem likely that the first decision provoked furious dissent and debate among committee members and, probably, among their friends rolling out on strike. The reversed decision indicates the tremendous volatility of the situation. And, secondly, both decisions firmly suggest that it was the strike wave which influenced the general strike call, not some desperate whim of a few leaders. Anxious and quixotic the rank and file leaders may well have been, but surely they must too have been elated by the tide running in their direction.

The third point is also interesting. The last sentence, quoted above, is word for word from a statement of the executive of the SDF issued in response to the strike manifesto, and, incidentally, also quoted verbatim by Tillett in his 1931 autobiography. Of course pre-existing organisation would have been desirable. But the very experience the movement was passing through was creating organisation out of struggle. At that point only the sectarians of the SDF including the leading figure Hyndman would not embrace this truth.

To return to Llewellyn Smith. According to his 'experienced eye' the daily processions 'had kept up the numbers', even if there were 'fewer and fewer dockers in their ranks'. He had also told us that 'numberless trades threw in their lot with the strikers and joined the processions.' This was the heady atmosphere in which the dockers' strike committee had met on 29 August. There is little doubt that for the future Sir Hubert Llewellyn Smith, soon to become first head of the Board of Trade Labour Department, a 'general strike' would indeed be 'a low water mark'.

Finally, there is the uncomfortable evidence that Engels opposed the general strike call. On 1 September he wrote to Laura Marx in France, '...it was threatening more than they could carry out, it was such a declaration of despair and such a desperate game that I wrote to Tussy at once..., fortunately they have thought better of it...'[78] He was certainly aware of the wave of strikes in London. It is possible that at the moment of his statement he was not aware of its scale. But for such an avid follower of detailed events that seems unlikely. There is a better explanation. Not since the Chartists in 1842 had the European workers' movement produced a similar situation: a series of struggles, a great upsurge in one industry and rolling actions by other workers. It was still a further 15 years before another great revolutionary thinker Rosa Luxemburg theorised on the process and importance of mass strikes in the revolutionary struggle. And that came *after* the English struggle of 1889, struggles in Germany and the great Russian Revolution of 1905.[79]

Some of this is speculative, but what is not is our knowledge of how the unionisation and strike movement progressed during that upsurge. Following the success at Beckton the union drive ran through most of London's gas works in the summer and autumn, though not with the success of Beckton. Other industries in east London were also affected, including the rubber industry of Silvertown, to the east of West Ham, where Eleanor Marx was active in the autumn. On 19 November it was reported, 'Some two hundred women marched up with the men to take part in a demonstration at Victoria Park. This marks a new and important feature in the history of trades unionism—the Union of women with men for common good. Silvertown is so remote that it has escaped general attention. Yet here some three thousand persons have been out on strike for nearly ten weeks, the women having struck for the sake of their male comrades.'[80]

The Silvertown dispute was a definite spin off from the dock strike and the action of the gas stokers. So was the battle for unionisation at the South Metropolitan Gas Company that same autumn. As both disputes broke out dockers and gas workers rallied round. The demonstrations and picket lines were supported. Donations were given and collections taken throughout the East End and further afield. Both were long and bitter struggles and both ended in defeat as employers regained their footing after the heady days of August and September. The manner of the ending of the dock strike, the ongoing battles on the docks and the closing down of the mass movement took a great toll on attempts to unionise in the immediate period which followed, especially in London. Beyond London the results were patchy with some successes.

The organising drive in the gas industry spread far and wide: to Cardiff, Wolverhampton, Sheffield, Manchester, Halifax, Hull, Tyneside and, most spectacularly, to Leeds. In the winter of 1889-90 Leeds gas workers joined up to the union *en masse* and obtained the eight hour day. The leaders of the municipal undertaking conceded but had a concealed plan to reinstate the 12 hour day and smash the union in the summer slack period. In June 1890 they tried to import hundreds of blacklegs to be protected by police and soldiers. Some sense of the workers' attitudes in the town is given by the attendance of over 6,000 on Leeds' first

May Day march. Present were nearly 1,000 gas workers, hundreds of builders' labourers who had formed a new union in the previous summer, and a large contingent of tailoring workers who had struck successfully in the autumn of 1888.

When the Council Gas Committee announced its 'new' arrangements a group of workers immediately struck and were followed two days later by almost the entire gas works labour force. The blacklegs who had arrived by rail were harassed by crowds of Leeds workers, estimated to be up to 30,000 strong, slugging it out with police in the streets. Those who did not leave town were guarded in the Town Hall. Ultimately they were marched out towards the gas works, escorted by a large force of police, foot soldiers and caribineers. A journalist reported the scene as they approached the railway bridges by the gas works:

> The bridges were crowded with men, who had stormed Holbeck station, made their way down the line and taken possession of them; and there they massed piles of missiles. In addition, the roofs of the buildings on either side of the road were covered with men who had also provided themselves with ammunition...the advanced guard was allowed to get under the bridges almost in safety. The victims the stone throwers wanted were the "knobsticks"... As they came within range, the fire was directed with terrific force on them, all who followed. The scene that ensued SIMPLY DEFIES DESCRIPTION, bricks, stones, "clinkers", iron belts, sticks, etc, were hurled into the air to fall with SICKENING THUDS AND CRASHES upon and amongst the blacklegs and their escorts.[81]

The scabs retreated. The council caved in. The union won.

There was also a roll-on effect on the waterfront from the London dock strike. Firstly in London itself victory was registered in a rash of waterfront disputes where employers were reluctant to accept the Mansion House Agreement. The euphoria of the famous meeting on Tower Hill addressed by John Burns on 19 September was shortlived. As workers returned they refused to work with scabs:

> The hostility of the union labourers to the blacklegs again took an acute form on Tuesday morning in the South West India Dock. The dock officials took in a number of casual hands. A large crowd of dockers gathered at the gates...and 150 of them were taken on. They began work, and there was apparently no intention of resenting the presence of the blacklegs, about 100 of whom were scattered about the dock, when...a signal was given...and the whole body left their work and bore down upon every blackleg that was inside...many of them being severely handled.[82]

There were many such reports and the anger of the dockers was intensified when many employers tried to renege on the Mansion House Agreement. Union leaders got a very bad reception when they attempted to persuade their members to stay at work under such conditions. At Hay's Wharf a four month strike started in January 1890 to defend dinner time payments. It was defeated but that did not deter several other unofficial actions along the waterfront.

Elsewhere seamen flocked to their new union and in

Southampton, Plymouth, Cardiff, Liverpool, Hull, Glasgow, Dundee and Dublin new dock worker unions rapidly emerged or slightly older ones grew in size. In Bristol New Unionism really caught on. *The Western Daily Press* reported long and bitter strikes among Somerset colliers at Radstock and Clandown.[83] And later a worker reminisced, 'The first strike occurred at Lysaght's Galvanised Iron Works and this was followed in varying succession by Tinn's Galvanised Iron Workers, the Gas Workers, Dockers, Stay Makers, Cotton Operatives, Brush Makers, Hatters, Oil and Colour Workers, Pipe Makers, Coal Carriers, Scavengers, Box Makers, Cigar Makers, Tramways Men, Hauliers, Blue Factory Workers, Animal Charcoal Workers, etc, etc.'[84]

In the north east of England the new mood preceded the upsurge in London. In July Northumberland miners protested against further grants to the royal family and followed with a demand for a 5 percent pay increase. Durham miners demanded 10 percent and an end to the sliding scale. Durham enginemen demanded 20 percent and Cleveland blastfurnacemen 4 percent. On 3 August in Sunderland the newly formed sailors and firemen's union claimed recruitment of 60,000 in one year with branches in 47 ports. Middlesborough dockers launched a union on 9 August and on the 13th Gateshead chain-makers proclaimed their support for all strikers. On the 19th Consett cokemen claimed 1,000 new members in the previous two weeks and the Newcastle based National Labour Federation announced 20 new branches and 'massive recruitment'.[85]

In Birmingham by the end of August several factories

were contributing to the London dockers' strike fund and 'a procession of trade unionists went through the streets with collecting sheets on handcarts. A large sum was collected and a proposal made to call a Birmingham General Strike!'[86]

And among craft unionists in Lancashire cotton workers registered the highest number of strikes in any industry. There were over 230 recorded in the year. Over 25 strikes are detailed in *The Cotton Factory Times* for the months of July, August and September in Burnley, Oldham, Bolton, Haslinden, Preston, Great Harwood, Failsworth, Bury, Rawtenstall, Blackburn, Chorley, Darwen, Royton and Earby. Some involved thousands of workers, most hundreds. They involved weavers and spinners, skilled and unskilled, men, women and children. The stated causes were wide ranging: underpayment of agreed prices, pay cuts, working hours, heavy handed supervision, victimisation. The paper, very much a tool of the union bureaucracy, is not warmly disposed to strikers. It is all too ready to spot the work of 'rowdy youths of 16-20' (27 September) and finds 'it pleasing to say they have all gone back' (6 September), but does communicate a sense of unrest — 'strikes of weavers in Burnley are recently very common' (30 August).[87]

There were also union drives among the unskilled in Dundee, Aberdeen and several places in West Yorkshire where the most notable was the Manningham Mills Strike in Bradford starting in the following year between December 1890 and April 1891. Over 5,000 struck in an attempt to resist wage cuts — involving a majority of female workers. It was truly a mass strike for thousands of workers were repeatedly in action during the five months supported on the streets by other Bradford workers. They fought the police for the right to march and hold meetings when the Mayor and Town Clerk banned them from both indoor and outdoor council owned venues. The strike ended in defeat.

The Manningham Mills dispute was the last major strike of this two year period. The defeat was one of several, as trade declined and the balance of forces tilted back to the employers. An employers' offensive had begun before the dock strike had ended. It became increasingly shrill as the movement had spread. Workers were once more faced with the hatred and disdain of the ruling class as they again faced the reality of mass unemployment.

At Bradford bitterness was sharpened by the knowledge that the mill's proprietor, Samuel Cunliffe Lister, was a leading figure in the Liberal Party and a self proclaimed benefactor of the people. He had 'modestly' claimed at the beginning of the dispute:

> I am proud to be able to say that if I have enriched myself I have also benefited thousands and have done more for the prosperity of the town of Bradford than any other man.[88]

It did not go down well. A similar realisation by Leeds workers, where the town council was Liberal, had been softened by the victory of the gas workers the previous year. The outcome of the Manningham Mills dispute was the single most important event in setting in train the shift from industrial struggle to independent labour electoral politics. The Independent Labour Party, launched from

Bradford in 1893, was in essence the West Yorkshire creation of socialist activists hoping to outflank their bosses electorally when their industrial struggle had foundered.

The TUC was to feel the fresh breeze of the unskilled upsurge. After its foundation in 1868 the organisation had sunk into a groove of complacency. It had become a British institution tolerated by most of the establishment and actively accepted by its Liberal wing. Its small craft union bureaucracies had settled into political life. Engels wrote, 'They are...model working men...and they are very nice people indeed nowadays to deal with, for any sensible capitalist in particular and for the whole capitalist class in general.'

John Burns recalled the impression made on him at the 1890 Congress:

> Physically the 'old' unionists were much bigger men than the 'new', and that, no doubt, is due to the greater intensity of toil during the last 20 or 30 years... The 'old' delegates differed from the 'new' not only physically but in dress. A great number of them looked like respectable city gentlemen; wore very good coats, large watch chains and high hats — and in many cases were of such splendid build and proportions that they presented an aldermanic, not to say a magisterial form and dignity. Amongst the 'new' delegates not a single one wore a tall hat. They looked workmen. They were workmen. They were not such sticklers for formality or Court procedure, but were guided more by common sense.[89]

The two main issues causing conflict were the eight hour day and the sliding scale of wages. The old guard believed, with their liberal economics teachers, that the economy would be wrecked if the state intervened on working hours or if trade unions ceased to tie wage levels to prices. Keir Hardie had introduced the eight hour question to the Bradford Congress of the TUC in 1888 where he sharply attacked the leadership. He was treated with disdain and heavily defeated. It was lost again in 1889. By 1890 the new unions were heavily represented. Affiliated membership had grown by 200,000 or 25 percent in one year. Congress resolved by 193 votes to 155, 'that the time had arrived when steps should be taken to reduce the working hours in all trades to eight per day...by Parliamentary enactments.' The leaders fought a strong rearguard action over the years which followed, but in essence a further step had been taken away from the embrace of *laissez faire* economics. It was the force of New Unionism which brought this about and its impact was strongly felt in the old unions too.

The new movement made itself felt on the streets too. On 4 May 1890 there took place in London the first May Day demonstration. Engels wrote for a German workers' paper:

> ...on 4 May 1890 the English proletariat, rousing itself from 40 years of hibernation, rejoined the movement of its class... Surrounding the seven platforms of the Central Committee were dense crowds as far as the eye could see, marching up with music and banners, over a hundred thousand in the procession, reinforced by almost as many who had come individually; everywhere harmony and enthusiasm, and yet order and organisation.[90]

Even the language of trade unionism was changing. The

ponderous 'bourgeois' English of the craft unions, aping the parliamentary language of their middle class friends, was replaced with down to earth plain English. The rules of the gas workers said:

> Trade Unionism has done excellent work in the past, and in it lies the hope of the Workers for the future; that is the Trade Unionism which clearly recognises that today there are only two classes, the producing Working Class and the possessing Master Class. The interests of these two classes are opposed to each other... [The Gasworkers are]...a union which embraces every kind of 'unskilled' labour and admits all workers, women, as well as men, on an equal footing.

And there was also a language ringing with the confident belligerence of some of the statements of the Chartist Mass Strike of 1842. The new Factory Operatives and General Labourers Union inscribed in its rule book an anti-scab charter which read:

> *BLACKLEGS OR SCABS*
>
> *All respectable members will avoid living, eating, drinking, walking, speaking or in any way encouraging these objectionable rags of society to exist to any extent in our midst.*[91]

A charter for now as well as the 1890s!

So the strike wave itself was characterised by some very distinctive features. It was unambiguously an upsurge of the unskilled, though many groups of skilled workers were infected, making their own demands. It brought forward a central demand, for the eight hour day, though not necessarily in each separate dispute. It was tremendously militant, each dispute usually involving thousands of workers and each one usually having the financial and often the physical backing of other workers in the town or area. There was often a complete lack of regard for the police, the soldiers and any other authority figures who stood in the movement's way. Its all embracing character drove straight in to the TUC shaking up the sectional attitudes of the leaderships of the craft unions. It provoked the employing class into a vicious determination to destroy what they saw as the desire 'to confiscate capital'. Finally, most of the disputes were led by men, and some women, from both inside and outside the industries, who were proud to declare themselves socialists. It was truly a mass movement at once spontaneous, unexpected, uneven, spirited, inventive and subject to very rapid and sudden changes of mood.

Part 4
Conclusion

For Frederick Engels New Unionism was about more than establishing trade unions for unskilled workers. In 1892 he wrote:

> The new unions were founded at a time when the faith in the eternity of the wages system was severely shaken; their founders and promoters were Socialists either consciously or by feeling; the masses whose adhesion gave them strength, were rough, neglected, looked down upon by the working class aristocracy; but they had this immense advantage, that their minds were virgin soil, entirely free from the inherited 'respectable' bourgeois prejudices which hampered the brains of the better situated 'old' unionists. And thus we see now these new unions taking the lead of the working class movement generally, and more and more taking in tow the rich and proud 'old' unions.[92]

What Engels had clearly observed in the events of 1888 to 1891 was the emergence of a new mass movement of workers coming together as a class, spearheaded by the 'rough' and 'neglected', pulling the more conservative elements behind them in a challenge to the 'eternity of the wages system'. Today we have the advantage over Engels of hindsight. We can see that the upsurge was checked; that, in decline, the new unions settled for defensive consolidation. And we can see that 'before the ink was dry on Engels' pen' most of the leading figures in this movement had exchanged the politics of picket line and mass demonstration for those of the electoral process.

Most commentators and historians have commended the pioneers on two counts. Making a virtue of necessity, they consolidated those gains they could and laid the basis for general trade unionism. Secondly, realising the limitations of the industrial struggle, they used the skills acquired in the struggle to move towards the creation of independent labour representation. Engels' notion that there had been the possibility of an aggressive anti-capitalist movement leading towards the building of a socialist society has been largely forgotten, a victim of the undeniable fact that socialism did not come about.

It is of course important to record what did happen. We must account for the actual course followed by the movement. But we must not lose sight of Engels' insight, for if he was right, an analysis of what went wrong could throw light on some every important questions which remain fresh and relevant today. They should include: how do mass movements appear and develop, how are they arrested and what part can conscious political activists play in the process?

New Unionism made a number of important advances. It extended trade unionism to sections of society which had been thought beyond organisation. These were the pawns of the labour market: men, women and children moving in and out of work at the whim of employer and trade cycle. It was thought that their permanent struggle for survival at wages around mere subsistence would never give them the space to think about collective action, let alone achieve it. Yet this constituency sprang forward throughout Britain in tens of thousands in a two year period. Will Thorne's memorable statement got through to people: 'It is easy to break one stick, but when 50 sticks are together in one bundle it is a much more difficult job.' New unions were formed. They spread. And despite enormous difficulty, they survived.

They were different from their predecessors. They opened the door to 'members unlimited' creating '...a union which embraces every kind of unskilled labour and admits all workers, women, as well as men, on an equal footing.' This was true, though circumstances dictated that some would organise within particular industries whilst others would be truly 'general', offering membership to anyone. They charged very low entry fees.

They were militant. In practice they learnt very quickly that they had to challenge obstinate employers and that mass picketing was absolutely necessary. Some, like the Leeds gas workers, showed that sometimes it would be necessary to go even further. They gave short shrift to scabs, 'the objectionable rags of society'. The implication of such activity demanded that their meagre funds should be available for strike support for their own members and for others. Unlike their skilled predecessors they should not be preoccupied with fringe benefits like sickness and burial funds.

Mann and Tillett put the argument clearly:

> The work of the trade unionist is primarily to obtain such a re-adjustment of conditions between employers and employed as shall secure to the latter a better share of the wealth they produce, in the form of reduced working hours and higher wages; and our experience has taught us that many of the older unions are very reluctant to engage in a labour struggle, no matter how great the necessity because they are hemmed in by sick and funeral claims...we, therefore advocate, strongly, the necessity, for labour organisations dealing with trade matters only.[93]

Whatever may have become of the leaders later, it must be said that they largely behaved with extraordinary physical and mental courage, great discipline and inspiring and creative determination in the face of potentially daunting problems. But the story cannot be left there.

Within a few years of 1889 those of the new unions that survived the state and employer offensive had shrunk in size and income. In some cases they had become exclusive. In the main they had retreated from their aggressive militancy, adopting much of the collaborative strategy of their older associates. Some had taken on the much criticised 'benefit' function. The seamen's union reeling from the brutal attacks of the Shipping Federation became violently anti-socialist, but most moved from militancy to the attempt to build an independent labour electoral organisation. Of the celebrated leaders of the struggle Tillett, Thorne, Sexton, Burns and Wilson became MPs, the latter two strongly pro-Liberal rather than Labour. Only Tom Mann of the industrial workers did not follow the route, though in 1892 he toyed with the idea of becoming a Church of England parson, a course much encouraged by Cardinal Manning![94] Instead he took on the secretaryship of the new ILP at the Bradford founding conference. He later founded another general union in 1898, the Workers' Union,[95] moving leftwards into syndicalism and ending in the new Communist Party in 1920.

Mann apart, it is tempting to see the behaviour of the others in terms of their 'flawed' personalities. Most of us are familiar with the condemnation of a deserting comrade. 'I always knew Ted was a villain, etc, etc...' With men like Tillett, Sexton and Burns it would be easy to malign them in terms of personal weakness, arrogance or vanity displayed early in their political lives. But this is not really satisfactory. No one has a negative word to say for Will Thorne. His behaviour seems to have been exemplary. Indeed his autobiography seems truthful and modest and very reliable as an account of what it took to build a union in difficult circumstances. Yet Thorne, no less than the others, became a right wing Labour MP and firm anti-communist. It is the interaction of individuals and circumstances which will usually determine the course to be taken. We must return to Engels.

Engels saw a rising mass movement. East London was the key, 'no longer a haunt of misery...the stagnant pool it was six years ago...It has shaken off its torpid despair, has returned to life...' In August 1889 it was in turmoil. Apart from the 60,000 strong dock strike and 10,000 strong tailors' strike the press informs us that there were dozens of stoppages flaring up, like 'tinder'.

It all came on the crest of a wave starting with the Match

Girls and moving to the gas stokers. The daily demonstrations criss-crossing the area and pushing out to the City and West End must have been an immense encouragement to the poor labourers struggling in their workshops for a pittance. But it is obvious too that the excitement did not stop at the edge of casual and unskilled work. The tailors were just the most voluble and actively charged craftsmen. There were engineers, plasterers, printers, and iron puddlers represented, as well as the multitude of crafts associated with shipbuilding. If this was what Engels was taking in, it is easy to see what led him to write, 'The revival of the East End of London remains one of the greatest and most fruitful facts of this *fin de siècle*, and glad and proud I am to have lived to see it.'

Yet the movement was not just about east London. The drive to unionisation spread to most parts of Britain. It was just as militant with a cutting edge of class identity. In Liverpool 'the sailors and firemen stormed the Sailors' Home, where the masters were enlisting rats, and drove them from their holes....despite the extra force of police, they have charged and routed a large number of rats.' In Leeds the gas stokers threw paving stones down on scabs and police. Thirty thousand Bradford people came out to enforce the Manningham Mill workers' right to demonstrate publicly. And it was the future red baiting John Havelock Wilson who was jailed for three months in Cardiff for organising pickets to deal with scabs in Cardiff Bay where the Shipping Federation was billeting them on the liner *Speedwell.* These are simply some of the best known events in a period exceptional in the incidence of militant actions nationwide.

However, it is also clear that they look like fragmentary and isolated incidents. Indeed, all these referred to occurred after the dock strike when hindsight at least, tells us the movement was in decline. Each of the events following the end of the strike took place in the context of a renewed offensive by the employers. There were fewer and fewer victories for the workers. Leeds apart, the gas workers tended to lose their battles, both in London and the provinces. The dock employers outside of London showed increasing resolution and those inside began to renege on the Mansion House Agreement.[96] Each little success for the employer led to greater confidence and a broadening offensive.

During the dock strike there was a definite sense of an example being followed in the rash of strikes reported for the latter half of August, in London at least. After the strike ended the records do not appear to yield up anything similar. Yet the strikers were said to have won. The London strikes on the riverside and in the gas works seem much more defensive, and much less successful. This turned out to be the case outside of London too with a few notable exceptions. The London strike had a positive effect upon Hull where the immediate union drive in the autumn of 1889 was almost completely successful. Yet the new organisation proved unable to resist the determined offensive mounted by the employers in 1892-93. In Southampton, Plymouth, Cardiff and Swansea the dockers failed, though in the latter there was compensatory recruitment among tinplate workers. In Liverpool initial success before the London strike was almost completely reversed in 1893 after years of defensive infighting in by the Dock Labourers' Union.

Given that east London was certainly the storm centre of the new movement it seems likely that its fate would be bound up with events there. The nature of the ending of the strike seems critical. Firstly the demands were so modest in relation to the strength of the mobilisation. The actual settlement by a group of 'wise men' from the establishment was so orderly, conducted so much in their terms, and so much out of sight of the workers. It is hardly surprising that a large chunk of that establishment presented it as a dockers' victory. It is clear that it came as a great relief to Cardinal Manning.

The great success of Manning and his committee was the settlement. But the telling moment which allowed the settlement to take place at all was surely the decision to reverse the general strike call. And the two things need to be considered together, for the one surely followed from the other. Broadening the struggle to include the other oppressed workers of east London, many of whom were already on strike, would certainly have disturbed the orderly progression from the Wade Arms to the Mansion House. It would also have allowed the movement outside of London to develop impetus and shape.

That the struggle was not broadened in August and that the initiative passed to the 'wise men' raises the question of the character of the strike's leadership. All of the leading figures were socialists. Most had spent half a decade in and around the East End making socialist propaganda and participating in the political campaigns: unemployment, free speech, the eight hours activity and Ireland. They had spoken on street corners, at factory gates and the docks. They had sold papers, addressed public meetings and organised and participated in demonstrations small and vast. They were well known figures in the area and were liable to be invited to help people in struggle as the non-dockers had been by Tillett and as all of them had been by the tailors. Their work, and that of the many socialist activists really does show the benefit of years of consistent and persistent work. Their consistency and effectiveness had earned them their place as leaders.

Tom Mann had been involved in assisting at several strikes in the 80s, and perhaps John Burns had some such experience, but no one had experience of being at the head of a mass strike movement; indeed none had been even involved in one before. No one else around had any such experience either. The last mass strike on any scale had been in 1842, in the year that Frederick Engels had come to Manchester. The socialist and labour movements therefore offered very little in the way of strategies for progressing big strikes. The socialist organisations still lacked clarity on the rather basic question of the role and value of trade unions.

The two main socialist papers, *Justice* and *Commonweal*, reported industrial struggles patchily but did not discuss strategy. Neither did they communicate any sense of excitement with the events happening on their doorsteps. On the contrary, *Justice* patronised the dock strikers: 'We congratulate the dockers on the very little modicum of success that has been obtained at so great a cost'.[97] By contrast the

Northern Star, in the late 1830s and 1840s, had bubbled with news of the Chartist movement and was redolent with class hatred and eagerly awaited by its readers.[98]

The socialist leaders of New Unionism were individuals taking individual initiatives and as such must have been vulnerable to self doubt and anxiety about consequences. It may well have been such doubts and anxieties which led to the retreat from the General Strike Manifesto on 30 August, an act making them specially vulnerable to the intervention of Cardinal Manning in early September, even if he had not been directly involved in the decision to retreat.

An honest assessment of the dock strike should acknowledge the victory in achieving its limited aims and establishing the right to organise, both enormous steps forward for the labour movement. But it should also be clear that, at the last moment, the initiative was seized by elements outside of the working class whose major goal was containment of the aspirations of the working class participants. The loss of this initiative proved to be very costly.

When the employers began their counter-assault, resistance was totally localised and fragmented. Victories were hard fought. There were few of them. Success was often temporary. They seem not to have inspired others to follow. Defeats were much more frequent and must have lowered morale, contributing nothing positive to future struggles. Within three years there were virtually no victories on the industrial front. The employers' offensive was a savage counter-attack. For the bosses ideas clarified quickly. A markedly harder set of attitudes became respectable in ruling circles. Even craft trades unions, condescendingly tolerated for 20 years, were now being seen as the class enemy. Tillett's new union was quite beyond the pale:

> [It]...cares not whether men are ill or well paid; it is ever ready with a fresh demand. Concession does but whet its appetite; it claims for labour the whole of the profits made by labour and capital combined; it aims to be the absolute dictator of the conditions of toil; to say who shall work and what he shall receive... The principle which underlies the militant union is the principle of socialism...it desires to confiscate capital.[99]

Something needed to be done. *The Times* led the charge. As early as Christmas Eve, 1889, it was advocating organised scabbing:

> Why should they (free labour or scabs) suffer themselves to be intimidated by a set of loud-voiced bullies, whose skins, we venture to say, are quite as tender as those of the honest men they coerce? The difference lies, we believe, in discipline and organisation. The bullies organise themselves, having nothing else to do, while the workers feel themselves isolated and undisciplined. Surely there is a function here for employers to discharge. They ought to take the lead in organising, disciplining, and encouraging men who wish to work. If picketing is legal...then so it must be legal to picket the pickets.[100]

In the early part of the dock strike the balance of opinion had been for the dock workers. The large meetings and processions, the mass pickets, the workers' unwillingness to accept the bosses' first offer, possibly the general strike call, even though it was revoked and the large donation from

Australian workers together shifted that opinion to outright hostility. The proprietors of the South West Metropolitan Gas Company's successful attack on Will Thorne's new union in December was acclaimed.

Over the decade of the 1890s the police and army would be further encouraged into a violently active role. Striking workers could be shot. At Featherstone in 1893 miners were. Employers were encouraged into vigorous resistance of union demands. Scab labour was actively organised and financed. — 50,000 cotton workers were locked out for ten weeks in 1893 and returned to a 5 percent wage reduction. The engineers were locked out in 1894, suffering a severe setback. The judiciary was encouraged to revise its interpretation of unions' legal rights. And it did. The culmination was the Taff Vale case in 1901 where the Amalgamated Society of Railway Servants and its exceedingly moderate leadership were held responsible for damages arising from a strike.

Violent aggression towards the organised labour movement was not the only response from within middle class circles. There were those who drew different conclusions from the events of 1889. A German observer writing only three years later marvelled at a movement 'originating not among the skilled and organised labourers, but among that hopeless 'Reserve Army of Industry' into whose ranks drift all those who have nothing to offer but the mere strength of their arms.'[101] He was astonished at 'the solidarity of the working classes and the force of public opinion'.[102] He attributed much of the success to the 'good sense' of the English workman, but more significantly to the active intervention of enlightened middle class people in the cause of social peace. And it was this kind of thinking which was important in the shift of the ruling class towards greater state intervention in social policy. In the guise of Fabianism this element was to have an enormous formative influence on the future ILP and Labour Party.

In the first instance though the employers' offensive was aggressive towards workers' organisation. Nevertheless the activists, now a decade or so in the movement, did not disappear, though Champion emigrated to Australia. Largely they pursued two complementary activities. Those in leadership roles in the new unions, locally or nationally, fought desperately to consolidate what they had got. This meant struggling to hold on to recruits and stabilising local branches by building less than grand bureaucracies, but bureaucracies nevertheless. And these bureaucracies would seek to restrain members from striking, as Tillett did when Hull dockers tried to save their new union in 1893. Strikes were costly. It was a matter of survival as much as principle. And since, away from the picket lines and strike committees, political differences between members could be wide, it was risky to be overtly political. The industrial and political spheres should be separate. This explains the future course of Will Thorne and James Sexton.

Thorne carried on his drive to build a union. As its first full time organiser and officer, heavy responsibility fell upon him for the day to day activity. Members who wanted to strike and fight were a problem rather than a gift. For a long time political activity was of secondary importance. He became an MP in 1906 for West Ham, the constituency where his original crusade to build the union had begun. Administering a union and sitting in William Morris's 'dung heap' dulled his fighting instincts. During the Great War he wore the uniform of a Lieutenant Colonel in the Volunteers, went to Russia in 1917 to try to persuade the Russians to keep fighting, having bitterly attacked German trade unionists who had come to Britain before the War to call for international resistance to war.

Sexton ran the Liverpool based National Union of Dock Labourers from 1893 till the merger with the T&G. More flamboyant than Thorne, his autobiography indicates his pleasure in mixing with the 'nobs' like Lord Derby, 'my good friend and former neighbour', with whom he attended Aintree Races in the 20s, in the company of the soon to be fascist-loving Prince of Wales.[103] He became MP for St Helens in 1918. His 'friend' Lord Derby described him as 'a very straight little man and not at all the sort to countenance Bolshevism'. Sexton became 'Sir James' in 1931.

The main lesson drawn by union leaders from 1889 was that militancy was a costly last resort in the face of ruthless employers supported by a hard faced state. The solution was to get hold of the state and change it. The means to do that was by getting workers' representatives into parliament and winning a parliamentary majority. Ben Tillett and John Burns were captivated by that strategy. Both were open to flattery. Both liked applause. Both enjoyed mixing with 'gentlemen' who showed them respect. Separated from the mass movement of 1889 their vanity, even useful to that movement, was unrestrained, although Tillett's flirtation with syndicalism in 1911 is proof that circumstances are critical in determining direction. Even right wing officials can be influenced by the attitude and activity of their members. Nevertheless Tillett became a great patriot and revelled in the company of ruling class villains like Churchill, Kitchener and Haig. He was 'commissioned' to visit the trenches in 1914-15 to listen to the soldiers and report back to the generals.

Burns never turned back to trade unionism. He liked the parliamentary life and it liked him. He was appointed to the Liberal Cabinet in 1906 but resigned at the outbreak of war, though continuing to help the war effort.

The first important steps in changing the movement's direction were taken at Bradford in 1893. In the wake of the terrible defeat of the Manningham Mills strikers the socialists who had played such a great part in support work turned away from the industrial struggle. The spirit of the founding conference of the ILP was a far cry from the rhetoric marking Tom Mann's position in spring 1890:

> If we trade unionists will steer clear of Parliament, with its thousand baneful influences, and pay honest and sole attention to our many duties as organised workmen and citizens, we shall press forward labour questions far more rapidly than by placing a value upon the gilded chamber of St Stephen's which never does a good thing except by outside compulsions and whose pernicious influences has [sic] emasculated a dozen or more honest workmen, rendering them well nigh impotent.[104]

From what the activists of 1893 perceived to be their isolation they sought to win support by diluting the language and activity of class struggle. The very first decision of the founding conference of the Independent Labour Party pointed towards deception and compromise. A majority of delegates agreed that to have the word 'socialist' in the new organisation's name would cut it off from large numbers of workers who did not consider themselves socialist. The long road to Ramsay MacDonald, Neil Kinnock and Tony Blair had begun.

We have been through the murky part of the story of New Unionism. But it would be wrong to leave the subject looking at the dark side. 1889 was unquestionably a milestone in the history of the labour and socialist movement. That the most downtrodden and oppressed members of the working class could take hold of their own destinies, however briefly, marked the re-entry of these groups into the world of political and industrial action. The source of the upturn was so unexpected and it inspired, or shamed, sections of the established movement into emulation. This was surely reflected in the massive attendance at the first May Day demonstration in 1890, an event neatly drawing together the militant upsurges in Britain and elsewhere with the founding of the Second International and its ringing call for the establishment of the eight hour day for workers everywhere.

That a few socialists, working tirelessly for years before the great events of 1888-89, could make a difference, in a situation written off as hopeless by so many, is a potent lesson for all activists at all times. The courage, fighting spirit and resolution of the Match Girls, averaging around 13 years of age, deserves the recognition accorded to the middle class suffragettes of the following decades. They surely deserve the last word:

> At the time of the strike...a girl was asked why it had taken place.
>
> "Well, it just went like tinder," she said; "one girl began, and the rest said 'yes', so out we all went".[105]

Notes

Introduction

1 Lucknow. It was characteristic of John Burns's populist rhetoric that he should compare the dockers' victory with a celebrated event in Victorian imperialist history. In the Indian Mutiny British troops were holed up in Lucknow for four months till relieved by a column of 5,000 troops.

2 See J Charlton, *The Chartists: The First National Workers' Movement* (London, 1997), Chapter 3.

The Match Girls

3 *The Link,* 23 June 1888.

4 *The Link,* 7 July 1888.

5 *The Link,* 14 July 1888.

6 Ibid.

7 *Justice,* 14 July 1888.

8 R Sampson, *Company History,* 1962, p51. *Bryant and May Company Papers,* D/B/BRY/1 at Hackney Archive, Hackney Library.

9 *The Link,* 23 June 1888.

10 M Harkness, *Out of Work,* cited in W J Fishman, *East End: 1888* (London, 1988), p51.

11 Anon, probably M Harkness, *British Weekly* Commissioners, *Toilers in London* (London, 1889), p176.

12 The only historian noting the connection is G Rose, 'The Strike at Bryant and May's Match Factory, East London, July 1888', in A Charlesworth, *An Atlas of Industrial Protest 1850-1900* (London, 1982), pp100-104.

13 G Rose, op cit, p102.

14 Cited in J A Jackson, 'The Irish in East London', *East London Papers,* vol 6, no 2 (December 1963), p112.

15 *1891 Census,* RG12/322/323/332.

16 *Strike Register,* compiled July 1888. Copies available at Tower Hamlets Local History Library and the TUC Library.

17 *The East End News,* 15 August 1882.

18 J Denvir, *The Irish in Britain* (London, 1891), p395.

19 *East London Advertiser,* 25 February 1888.

20 Related by Bryant at the half-yearly shareholders meeting, in September 1888 and in the correspondence between him and George Shipton. *Bryant and May Company Papers,* op cit, D/B/BRY/1/2/538-49;552-564.

21 One example: whilst he was making belligerent statements to the press about his fair play he was writing to other East End employers asking for their wage rates 'in strictest confidence'. *Bryant and May Company Papers,* op cit, letter book for 1888, D/B/BRY/1/2/552-564.

22 *Bryant and May Company Papers,* op cit, drama file D/B/BRY/1/2/538-49.

23 *The Link,* noted in August-October issues of the paper. There is a useful account of the post-strike situation in London in W J Fishman, op cit, pp284-302.

24 B Tillett, *Memories and Reflections* (London, 1931), pp106,108.

From Match Girls to dock strike

25 Residence and occupation confirmed by reading the 1891 Census for these districts. See note 15. For the flavour of community see A Davin, *Growing Up Poor: Home, School and Street in London 1870-1914* (London, 1996).

26 W Thorne, *My Life's Battles* (London, 1989), pp47-48.

27 Ibid, p76.

28 Ben Tillett, cited in D Torr, *Tom Mann and his Times,* vol 1 (1956), p281.

29 See chapter 5.

30 H Llewellyn Smith and V Nash, *The Story of the Dockers' Strike,* (London, nd), 1889-90, pp84-86.

31 H H Champion, *The Great Dock Strike in London: August 1889* (London, 1890), p169.

32 Ibid, p129.

33 B Tillett, op cit, pp112-113.

34 *Newcastle Daily Chronicle,* 27 August 1889.

35 Will Thorne, cited in D Torr, op cit, vol 1, p 287.

36 H Llewellyn Smith and V Nash, op cit, p83.

37 Ibid, pp94-95.

38 Ibid, p126.

39 Ben Tillett, cited in D Torr, op cit, p284.

40 T Mann, *Tom Mann's Memoirs* (London, 1967), p85.

Social and economic conditions

41 B Webb (Potter), 'The Docks', in C Booth, *Life and Labour of the People in London,* First Series 4 (London, 1904), pp17-18. Beatrice Webb and her husband Sydney were obsessive investigators of social conditions.

42 W Thorne, op cit, p18.

43 Cited in J Burnett, *Plenty and Want* (London, 1979), p206.

44 Robert Blatchford, 1889, cited in J Burnett, *A Social History of Housing* (London, 1978), p172.

The socialists

45 George was no socialist. His reputation among socialists was very much tarnished in 1887 when he joined the vitriolic attacks on the Haymarket Martyrs. See below and E P Thompson, *William Morris: Romantic to Revolutionary* (London, 1959), pp591-595.

46 J Prebble, *The Highland Clearances* (London, 1965).

47 M Chase, *The People's Farm* (London, 1983).

48 J L Mahon, cited in M Crick, *The History of the Social Democratic Federation* (Keele, 1994), p38.

49 The Fabian Society, founded in 1884, was composed largely of upper and middle class men and women. Its policy was to permeate the state and political parties to bring about social reform from above. Its members generally had no faith in the ability, or likelihood, of the working class to take action on its own behalf. The ideas of Fabianism certainly permeated the future Labour Party, wedding it to the notion of 'the inevitability of gradualism.'

50 Cited in C Tsuzuki, *HM Hyndman and British Socialism* (Oxford, 1961), p52.

51 E P Thompson, op cit, p481.

52 Ibid, p484.

53 Ibid, p576.

54 J W Mackail, *The Life of William Morris*, vol 2 (London, 1912), p203.

55 J L Mahon, cited in E P Thompson, op cit, p516.

56 Ibid, p521.

57 P A Watmough, 'The Membership of the Social Democratic Federation 1885-1902', *Bulletin of the Society for Labour History,* no 34, 1977, p38.

58 T Mann, *What a Compulsory Eight Hour Working Day Means to the Workers* (London, 1972), p26.

59 W Morris, *Commonweal,* 7 September 1889.

60 William Morris, letter to C E Maurice, 1883, cited in A Briggs, *William Morris: Selected Writings and Designs* (Harmonsdworth, 1968), p137.

61 E P Thompson, op cit, p602.

62 Engels to Sorge, February 1890 in F Engels, *Letters to Americans* (New York, 1963), p224.

The Irish

63 See J Newsinger, *Fenianism in Mid-Victorian Britain* (London, 1994).

64 Michael Davitt, quoted in T W Moody, 'Michael Davitt and the British Labour Movement 1882-1906', in *Transactions of the Royal Historical Society*, Fifth Series, vol 3 (1953), pp63-64.

65 Another helpful clue is provided by adverts for demonstrations in *Justice* and *Commonweal*. For example in the issue of 13 July, 1888, (during the Match Girls' Strike), *Justice* lists assembly points for an Anti-Sweating demonstration to take place the following week. Out of 12 places half are in the centre of London's Irish population, eg Canning Town, Burdett Road, Mile End Waste, Whitechapel Road, Commerical Street (incidently, all areas where the Match Girls lived) and Clerkenwell Green.

66 G Lansbury, *My Life* (London, 1928), p64.

67 Llewellyn Smith, cited in E J Hobsbawm, *Labour's Turning Point: 1880-1900* (London, 1974), p30.

68 For London, see P Thompson, *Socialists, Liberals and Labour: The Struggle for London 1885-1914* (London, 1967), p25, and for Liverpool, P J Waller, *Democracy and Sectarianism: A Political and Social History of Liverpool 1868-1939* (Liverpool, 1981), p26.

69 Cited in L H Lees, *Exiles of Erin: Irish Migrants in Victorian London* (Massachusetts, 1979), p211.

70 A phrase used by Trotsky to describe the attitude of the Russian proletariat towards Tsarism in 1917.

Runaway consciousness

71 H Llewellyn Smith and V Nash, op cit, pp73-76.

72 B Tillett, op cit, p141.

73 It raises the possibility that Tillett was simply copying from that newspaper when he wrote his autobiography.

74 R Gray, *Cardinal Manning* (London, 1992), p307, but also Shane Leslie, 'Cardinal Manning and the London Dock Strike of 1889', *Dublin Review* (1920), pp218-231. 'On August 30th, Miss Harkness brought Manning word from the strikers. "Half an hour later," she wrote, "I saw Cardinal Manning. Then I went away to fetch a list of Dock Directors. When I came back he was saying Mass. After that I had the satisfaction of seeing

him drive off in his carriage to the City".'

75 W L Fishman, *East End Jewish Radicals 1875-1914* (London, 1975), p197 for a full account of the tailors' strike.

76 In the London dock strike there were hundreds of enterprises, 150,000 strikers and 15,000 active pickets. Sources: reports in national and local newspapers; autobiographies. Since the 'incidents' are trawled from chance reports in newspapers it would be safe to assume many more and certainly a strike wave by any standard. Burnett reported over 2,000 disputes in cotton alone. My rough computation is that on 1 September 1889, perhaps 300,000 London workers were on strike. The newspapers from which the strike information was culled are: *The Times, Manchester Guardian, The Daily News, The East London Advertiser, The East London News, The East London Observer, The Newcastle Daily Chronicle* and the *Western Daily News.* See the list of strikes in the east London area below.

List 1

Strikes taking place within the 'triangle' referred to on page 98.

Eyre & Spotiswoode—printers
Waterlow and Sons (up to 4 sites)—paper manufacturers
Jukes, Coulson, Stokes—export iron mongers
McDougall's—millers
Pickfords—carters (up to 9 sites)
Crosse & Blackwells—jam factory
Thomas Whinall—jam factory
Johnson Bros—waterproof clothing
Joseph Davis—rope, linen and tarpaulin manufacturers
Frosts—rope makers
Copenhagen—oil mills
Westwood Baillie—iron works
Thames Iron Works, Blackwall
Chemical, Copper, Ore and Phosphate Co
Bryant and May—match makers
Railway coal depots at Liverpool Street, Finsbury, Kings Cross, Camden, St Pancras, Euston and Marylebone
Atlas Chemical
Fardell & Co—car-men
Army & Navy Stores—trunk makers
Charringtons Brewery
Plumstead sewage works
Coal heavers at South Metropolitan Gas Works
Also on strike in the area: sea-going engineers and fitters, boiler makers, carpenters, painters and decorators, shipwrights, iron ship builders, and caulkers

List 2

Strikes taking place outside of the 'triangle'

Peak Frean—biscuit makers, Bermondsey
Lloyds tinplate works, Bermondsey
Billingsgate fish porters
George Smith—saw mills, Pimlico
Thomas Hobbs—dust contractors, Paddington
Providence Iron Works, Millwall
Cutlery works, Millwall
Simpson & Co—engineers, Pimlico
Maudsleys—engineers, Pimlico
Parker & Lambert—coal merchants, Lambeth
Builders at Woolwich Arsenal
Laundry workers, Lambeth

In his report to the Board of Trade, *Strikes and Lock Outs in 1889*, John Burnett records the following: strikes in London (without the dock strike)—78, including 11 in engineering. This must surely be an underestimate.

77 *Newcastle Daily Chronicle,* 27 August 1889, and other papers.

78 F Engels and P Lafargue *Correspondence* (Moscow), vol II, pp306-307.

79 R Luxemburg, *The Mass Strike* (London, 1994), chs 6 and 7.

80 *East End News,* 19 November 1889.

81 Cited in H Hendrick, 'The Leeds Gas Strike 1890', *Thoresby Society: Miscellany* (1974), p88.

82 *The East London Advertiser,* 21 September 1889.

83 *Western Daily Press,* 27/28 August 1889.

84 S Bryher, 'Labour and Socialist Movement in Bristol', *Bristol Labour Weekly*, June 1929, p20.

85 *Newcastle Daily Chronicle* and the *Newcastle Journal and North Mail,* daily reports in the July and August issues.

86 *Manchester Guardian,* 2 September 1889.

87 *Cotton Factory Times* (1889). I am very grateful to Rachel Aldred of Manchester SWP for her trawl of this paper and the very perceptive remarks she has made.

88 C Pearce, *The Manningham Mills Strike, Bradford December 1890-April 1891* (Hull, 1975), p4.

89 John Burns 1890, cited in R Postgate, *The Builders History* (London, 1923), p343.

90 K Marx and F Engels, *Collected Works,* vol 27 (Moscow, 1990), p65.

91 E J Hobsbawm, *Labour's Turning Point* (London, 1974), p95.

Conclusion

92 F Engels, preface to the 1892 English Edition of *The Condition of the Working Class in England,* in *Marx and Engels on Britain* (Moscow, 1962), p32.

93 T Mann and B Tillett, *The 'New' Trades Unionism* (London, 1890).

94 J White, *Tom Mann* (Manchester, 1991), p75.

95 R Hyman, *The Workers' Union* (London, 1971).

96 Already by the autumn of 1889 the dock employers were insisting on employing who they liked. Tom Mann as president of the new union wrote several times to the employers demanding that they honour the spirit of the agreement. See J White, op cit, p50.

97 *Justice,* 21 September 1889.

98 M O'Brien, *'Perish the Privileged Orders', A Socialist History of the Chartist Movement* (London, 1995), pp97-99.

99 Edmund Vincent, cited in J Saville, 'Unions and Free Labour: Background to Taff Vale Decision', in A Briggs and J Saville, *Essays in Labour History* (London, 1967), p322.

100 Ibid, p323.

101 G von Schulze-Gaevernitz, *Social Peace: A Study of the Trade Union in England* (London, 1893), p251.

102 Ibid, p252.

103 J Sexton, *Sir James Sexton, Agitator: The Life of the Dockers' MP, An Autobiography* (London, 1936), p292.

104 Cited by J White, op cit, p55.

105 *British Weekly* Commissioners, *Toilers in London* (London, 1889), p176.

Index

REDWORDS